Using the Standards
Building Grammar & Writing Skills

Grade 3

by
Kathleen Hex

Published by Instructional Fair
an imprint of
Frank Schaffer Publications®

Instructional Fair

Author: Kathleen Hex
Editor: Stephanie Oberc

Frank Schaffer Publications®

Instructional Fair is an imprint of Frank Schaffer Publications.

Send all inquiries to:
Frank Schaffer Publications
3195 Wilson Drive NW
Grand Rapids, Michigan 49544

Using the Standards: Building Grammar & Writing Skills—grade 3

ISBN: 0-7424-1803-0

4 5 6 7 8 9 10 PHXBK 08 07 06 05 04

Introduction

The standards developed by the National Council of Teachers of English are a set of content guidelines to help educators ensure that every student reaches appropriate milestones and achieves success. Designing curriculum that helps students meet these standards can be challenging. *Using the Standards: Building Grammar & Writing Skills, Grade 3* will be a valuable asset to your writing program.

The activities and worksheets in this book are practical applications of the skills necessary to meet the NCTE standards. These pages can be seamlessly integrated into your existing curriculum and used for extension, reinforcement, enrichment, or review of the skills you are already teaching.

The book is divided into four components: language mechanics, usage, writing strategies, and writing applications. Language mechanics includes practice in capitalization, punctuation, and other rules of English. The usage activities center around common usage for elementary students, including subject-verb agreement and the correct use of nouns, pronouns, adjectives, verbs, and adverbs. Writing strategies help students understand the essential elements of writing and the writing process, such as clear and coherent sentences, paragraph structure, and maintaining consistent focus. The writing application section allows students to experience the writing process in a variety of genres. They will demonstrate their skills in friendly letters, expository writing, creative writing, and responses to literature.

Building the grammar and writing skills of your students will help them to meet the standards and provide a strong foundation for success in all content areas.

English Language Arts Standards

1. Read a wide range of texts.

2. Read a wide range of literature.

3. Apply a variety of strategies to comprehend and interpret texts.

4. Use spoken, written, and visual language to communicate effectively.

5. Use a variety of strategies while writing and use elements of the writing process to communicate.

6. Apply knowledge of language structure and conventions, media techniques, figurative language, and genre to create, critique, and discuss texts.

7. Research issues and interests, pose questions, and gather data to communicate discoveries.

8. Work with a variety of technological and other resources to collect information and to communicate knowledge.

9. Understand and respect the differences in language use across cultures, regions, and social roles.

10. Students whose first language is not English use their first language to develop competencies in English and other content areas.

11. Participate in a variety of literary communities.

12. Use spoken, written, and visual language to accomplish purposes.

© McGraw-Hill Children's Publishing

0-7424-1803-0 *Building Grammar & Writing Skills*

Table of Contents	Standards Reflected	Page
Introduction		3
Grammar: Capitalization		
School Days	4, 6	9
Who's Who	4, 6	10
Wish You Were Here	4, 6	11
It's a Boy!	4, 6	12
Geography Lesson	4, 6	13
Happy Holidays	4, 6	14
Grammar: Punctuation		
Saturday Matinee	4, 6	15
A Birthday Wish	4, 6	16
All in a Row	4, 6	17
My Grandpa	4, 6	18
The Treehouse	4, 6	19
Tricky Titles	4, 6	20
A Dog Day	4, 6	21
Hall of Fame	4, 6	22
Usage: Parts of Speech		
Tennis, Anyone?	4, 6	23
Peggy Fleming	4, 6	24
Three-Ring Circus	4, 6	25
Many Families	4, 6	26
Exceptional Nouns	4, 6	27
Half a Loaf	4, 6	28
Desert Treasures	4, 6	29
Fast Food Fun	4, 6	30
A Day at the Beach	4, 6	31
Being Me	4, 6	32
Helping Our Earth	4, 6	33
Rainy Day Fun	4, 6	34
Trip to the Mall	4, 6	35
Verb Matchup	4, 6	36
Shark Tank	4, 6	37
In Possession	4, 6	38
Describe It	4, 6	39
Making Comparisons	4, 6	40
Adventurous Adverbs	4, 6	41

© McGraw-Hill Children's Publishing

0-7424-1803-0 *Building Grammar & Writing Skills*

Table of Contents	Standards Reflected	Page

© McGraw-Hill Children's Publishing

0-7424-1803-0 *Building Grammar & Writing Skills*

Table of Contents	Standards Reflected	Page

© McGraw-Hill Children's Publishing 0-7424-1803-0 *Building Grammar & Writing Skills*

Table of Contents	Standards Reflected	Page

© McGraw-Hill Children's Publishing　　　　0-7424-1803-0 *Building Grammar & Writing Skills*

Name _____ Date _____

School Days

The first word in a sentence should begin with a capital letter.

Read each sentence. Underline with three short lines the first letter of each word that needs a capital letter. Rewrite the word correctly.

Example: Today <u>today</u> is the first day of school.

1. _____ sam takes the bus to school.

2. _____ the children play soccer at recess.

3. _____ everyone has fun reading a story.

4. _____ when will we do a science experiment?

5. _____ lunch is served in the cafeteria.

6. _____ our principal came to visit our class.

7. _____ students should be quiet in the library.

8. _____ the teacher writes the homework on the board.

9. _____ clean your desk before you go home.

10. _____ have a great day.

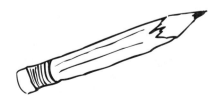

9

Name _____ Date _____

Who's Who?

The names of people begin with a capital letter.
The pronoun *I* is written as a capital letter.

Read each sentence. Underline with three short lines
the first letter of each word that needs a capital letter.
Write each sentence correctly.

Example: The librarian helped tracy find a book about susan b. anthony.

The librarian helped Tracy find a book about Susan B. Anthony.

1. i learned that george washington was the first president.

_____

2. matthew and amelia are doing a project about thomas jefferson.

_____

3. elisa and i are studying about abraham lincoln.

_____

4. harriet tubman helped rescue many people from slavery.

_____

5. Many people admire helen keller's courage and intelligence.

_____

6. Can i write a report about jackie robinson?

_____

0-7424-1803-0 *Building Grammar & Writing Skills*

Name _____ Date _____

Wish You Were Here

A **proper noun** names a special person, place, or thing.
Capitalize the first letter in each word of a proper noun.

Examples: california adventure = California Adventure
malibu = Malibu

Help Roberta correct her postcard. Underline with three short lines the first letter of each word that needs a capital letter.

Dear trudy,

My family and I are in los angeles california. We have been to hollywood, santa monica beach, and rodeo drive in beverly hills. Tomorrow we are going to visit disney land. I hope I will get to meet mickey mouse. Wish you were here,

Your friend,

roberta

Trudy Little
3501 Courtland
Garden City, KS
67846

Rewrite Roberta's postcard correctly.

_____

_____

_____

_____

11

Name _____ Date _____

It's a Boy!

Capitalize the first letter in the months of the year, days of the week, titles of respect, and abbreviations of titles of respect.

Examples: january = January   tuesday = Tuesday

doctor jones = Doctor Jones   mrs. clark = Mrs. Clark

Read the story below. Underline with three short lines the first letter of each word that needs a capital letter. Rewrite the story correctly.

My baby brother, Nicholas, was born on sunday, september 8, 2002. On saturday, my mom went to see doctor nelson at the hospital. Our neighbors, mr. and mrs. Bigelow, let me sleep over at their house. My mom and Nicholas came home on monday.

_____

_____

_____

_____

_____

_____

_____

12

0-7424-1803-0 *Building Grammar & Writing Skills*

Name _____ Date _____

Geography Lesson

Capitalize the first letter of each word in geographical names
and historical periods.

Examples: pacific ocean = Pacific Ocean
renaissance = Renaissance

Read each word. If the word should begin with a capital letter,
rewrite it correctly on the line.

1. rocky mountains _____

2. lake superior _____

3. ocean _____

4. kenya _____

5. country _____

6. middle ages _____

7. dinosaur _____

8. north pole _____

9. stone age _____

10. river _____

11. jurassic period _____

12. nile river _____

13. europe _____

14. state _____

15. atlantic ocean _____

0-7424-1803-0 *Building Grammar & Writing Skills*

Name _____ Date _____

Happy Holidays

Capitalize the first letter of each word
in the names of holidays and special events.

Read each sentence. Underline with three short lines
the first letter of each word that needs a capital letter.
Rewrite each sentence correctly.

1. Did you watch the rose parade on new year's day?

_____

_____

2. The librarian helps us choose books during national book week.

_____

3. My family eats turkey and potatoes on thanksgiving day.

_____

4. The class planted a tree on arbor day.

_____

5. Our christmas tree is decorated with lights and ornaments.

_____

6. We watched fireworks at the park on independence day.

_____

0-7424-1803-0 *Building Grammar & Writing Skills*

Name _____ Date _____

Saturday Matinee

A **sentence** is a group of words that tells a complete thought.

A sentence that tells something ends with a period. **(.)**
A sentence that asks a question ends with a question mark. **(?)**
A sentence that shows strong feeling ends with an exclamation point. **(!)**
A sentence that gives a command ends with a period. **(.)**

Read each sentence. Add the correct punctuation mark to the end of the sentence.

1. Do you want to go to the movies on Saturday ____

2. We are going to the theater at the mall ____

3. I am going to buy a large popcorn and a bag of candy ____

4. What do you like to eat at the movies ____

5. This movie is great ____

6. Meet me outside ____

Write four sentences of your own about a movie you have seen.
Try to include at least two different kinds of sentences.

_____

_____

_____

_____

     0-7424-1803-0 *Building Grammar & Writing Skills*

A Birthday Wish

A **sentence** is a group of words that tells a complete thought.

A sentence that tells something ends with a period. **(.)**
A sentence that asks a question ends with a question mark. **(?)**
A sentence that shows strong feeling ends with an exclamation point. **(!)**
A sentence that gives a command ends with a period. **(.)**

Write a story about a birthday wish. The story can be real or make believe. Try to use at least one of each kind of sentence. Make sure each sentence begins with a capital letter and ends with a punctuation mark.

_____

_____

_____

_____

_____

_____

_____

_____

_____

Name _____ Date _____

All in a Row

Use **commas (,)** to separate three or more items in a series.
   Example: spoons, forks, and knives

Read each sentence. Put commas in the correct places.

  1. Benjamin is wearing a tie coat and shoes.

  2. Talisa is wearing a swimsuit hat and sunglasses.

  3. Julia is shopping for pens pencils and erasers.

  4. She selects blue pens purple pencils and green erasers.

  6. Min is taking a trip to Washington Oregon and California.

  7. He will pack toys clothes and books in his suitcase.

  8. John Devon and Mitchell are going to the skate park.

  9. Mitchell makes sure to wear his helmet elbow pads and kneepads.

10. Skateboards in-line skates and roller skates are allowed in the skate park.

11. My parents my sister and I went to the symphony hall to see a concert.

12. We heard violins trumpets cellos pianos and drums.

13. Keisha Sandra and Travis are at the bowling alley for Juan's birthday party.

14. They are eating hot dogs pizza cake and ice cream.

15. Juan received a yo-yo a tennis racket and a soccer ball for his birthday.

   0-7424-1803-0 *Building Grammar & Writing Skills*

Name _____ Date _____

My Grandpa

Use a **comma** after the day in a date. But do not put a comma after the month
if no day is used.

  Example: May 12, 2002   May 2002

Use a comma after each part of an address.

  Example: 123 Main Street, Seattle, Washington

Use a comma between the city name and the state name when used together.

  Example: Seattle, Washington

Here is a story with commas in all the wrong places.
Rewrite the story putting the commas in the correct places.

   My grandpa had a very interesting life! He was born on, August, 20 1943.
He grew up in, Boston Massachusetts. In January, 1963, he moved to, Los Angeles
California. My grandpa lived at 349, James Street Los Angeles California. On
June, 8, 1964, he married my grandma at a church in, San Francisco California.
My dad was born on, February 1 1966.

_____

_____

_____

_____

_____

_____

_____

_____

18

Name _____ Date _____

The Tree House

Use a **comma** after the greeting and closing in a friendly letter.

Greeting: **Closing:**
Dear Teresa,   Your friend,
                      Samantha

Put commas in the correct places in the letter below.

Dear Donavan
    I can hardly wait to get to your house this
weekend. My dad will be dropping me off on
Saturday afternoon. We will have fun sleeping
in your tree house. Can we build a campfire?
                Your friend
                Simon

Write your own letter to a friend.

0-7424-1803-0 *Building Grammar & Writing Skills*

Name _____ Date _____

Tricky Titles

Titles of books are underlined when you write them by hand. When they are typed, titles of books are underlined or in italics.

    Examples: <u>James and the Giant Peach</u>
                     James and the Giant Peach

Titles of stories, poems, and songs are always in quotation marks.

    Examples: "Sleeping Beauty" (story)
                     "Paul Revere's Ride" (poem)
                     "Blue Suede Shoes" (song)

Read each sentence. Underline the title of a book.
Put quotation marks around the title of a story, poem, or song.

1. Luis read Number the Stars for his book report.

2. Stanley the Fierce is a poem by Judith Viorst.

3. Laura Ingalls Wilder wrote Little House in the Big Woods.

4. Our class sang America the Beautiful for the veterans.

5. The Gift of the Magi is a story sometimes told at Christmas.

6. Do you know how to play Happy Birthday on the piano?

7. A Girl's Garden is a poem by Robert Frost.

8. Last week I checked out Because of Winn-Dixie from the library.

9. My dad read us the story Tom Thumb before we went to sleep.

10. Our class is reading Sarah, Plain and Tall this month.

20

 0-7424-1803-0 *Building Grammar & Writing Skills*

Name _____ Date _____

A Dog Day

Read the story below. Underline with three short lines the first letter of any word that needs a capital letter. Put commas, periods, question marks, and exclamation points in the correct places. Write an ending to the story.

on october 19 2002 i went to the animal shelter to get a pet

my mom drove me to 171 main street huntsville texas we met mr

maxwell johnson he showed me cats dogs and rabbits that needed

to be adopted what kind of animal should i get

i noticed a small fluffy brown dog sitting quietly in the kennel

wow i knew that was the dog for me mr johnson helped the dog out

of the kennel, and she ran straight to me what should i name her

_____

_____

_____

_____

_____

_____

_____

0-7424-1803-0 *Building Grammar & Writing Skills*

Name _____ Date _____

Hall of Fame

Read the letter below. Underline with three short lines the first letter of
any word that needs a capital letter. Put commas, periods, question marks,
and exclamation points in the correct places. On the back of this paper,
write your own friendly letter about a place you have visited.

dear mrs ono

    my family and i went to cooperstown new york we visited the

baseball hall of fame it was terrific i saw the scorebook from roberto

clemente's last game a glove used by hank aaron and a plaque

honoring joe dimaggio i thought babe ruth was the most interesting

player to learn about did you know he was born in baltimore

maryland on february 6 1895 i wrote a poem about him called

george the babe i'll read it to the class when i get back on monday

              your student

              josh

0-7424-1803-0 *Building Grammar & Writing Skills*

Name _____ Date _____

Tennis, Anyone?

A **noun** names a person, place, or thing.

Underline the nouns in each sentence. Then find and circle the nouns in the Word Search. **Hint:** Words can go across, down, or backward.

1. Tennis is my favorite sport.

2. Maurice and I play at the park every Saturday.

3. There are three courts.

4. Each one has a net, a fence, and some lights.

5. My dad bought me a new racket.

6. I need some new shoes, too.

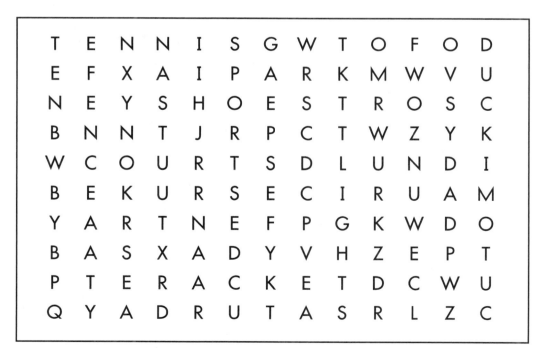

T	E	N	N	I	S	G	W	T	O	F	O	D
E	F	X	A	I	P	A	R	K	M	W	V	U
N	E	Y	S	H	O	E	S	T	R	O	S	C
B	N	N	T	J	R	P	C	T	W	Z	Y	K
W	C	O	U	R	T	S	D	L	U	N	D	I
B	E	K	U	R	S	E	C	I	R	U	A	M
Y	A	R	T	N	E	F	P	G	K	W	D	O
B	A	S	X	A	D	Y	V	H	Z	E	P	T
P	T	E	R	A	C	K	E	T	D	C	W	U
Q	Y	A	D	R	U	T	A	S	R	L	Z	C

0-7424-1803-0 *Building Grammar & Writing Skills*

Name _____ Date _____

Peggy Fleming

A **common noun** names any person, place, or thing.
Common nouns do not begin with a capital letter unless they are the first word
in a sentence.

    Examples: skater, ice

A **proper noun** names a special person, place, or thing.
Proper nouns begin with a capital letter.

    Examples: Peggy Fleming, Michelle Kwan

Read the story. Circle each common noun and underline each proper noun.

    Peggy Fleming is a famous figure skater. She was born in San Jose, California, and began skating when she was nine years old. She won many junior figure skating competitions as a child. In 1964, Peggy competed in the Winter Olympics in Austria. She took sixth place.

    Peggy's training in ballet helped her develop artistic skating routines. This helped her win a gold medal in the 1968 Winter Olympics in France.

    Peggy retired from amateur skating after the Olympics. She became a professional skater and toured the country doing ice shows. Now, Peggy is a commentator for television.

0-7424-1803-0 *Building Grammar & Writing Skills*

Name _____ Date _____

Three-Ring Circus

A **noun** names a person, place, or thing.
A **singular noun** names one person, place, or thing.
A **plural noun** names more than one person, place, or thing.

Add *s* to change most singular nouns to plural nouns.

    Example: dog = dogs

Add *es* to singular nouns that end in *sh, ch, s, x,* or *z*
to make them plural.

    Example: wish = wishes

Circle the correct spelling of the plural noun.

1.	elephant	elephants	elephantes
2.	box	boxes	boxs
3.	drum	drumes	drums
4.	clown	clownes	clowns
5.	swing	swings	swinges
6.	horse	horses	horsees
7.	tent	tentes	tents
8.	ticket	tickets	ticketes
9.	costume	costumees	costumes
10.	bicycle	bicycles	bicyclees
11.	flash	flashs	flashes
12.	announcer	announceres	announcers
13.	trampoline	trampolines	trampolinees
14.	punch	punches	punchs
15.	cannon	cannones	cannons

25

0-7424-1803-0 *Building Grammar & Writing Skills*

Name _____ Date _____

Many Families

A **plural noun** names more than one person, place, or thing.
Add *s* to change most singular nouns to plural nouns.

    Example: bag = bags

Add *s* to singular nouns ending in vowel-*y*.

    Example: key = keys

Change the *y* to *i* and add *es* to singular nouns
ending in consonant-*y*.

    Example: berry = berries

Change these singular nouns to plural nouns.

1. family _____
2. agency _____
3. pansy _____
4. monkey _____
5. bunny _____
6. therapy _____
7. valley _____
8. pantry _____
9. jury _____
10. kidney _____

11. baby _____
12. fly _____
13. penny _____
14. jelly _____
15. lady _____
16. turkey _____
17. tray _____
18. posy _____
19. journey _____
20. jetty _____

0-7424-1803-0 *Building Grammar & Writing Skills*

Name _____ Date _____

Exceptional Nouns

Some **plural nouns** have special spellings.

Example: child = children

Some nouns stay the same when plural.

Example: deer = deer

Write the plural form of each noun. Use a dictionary to help you.

I. tooth _____

2. goose _____

3. woman _____

4. child _____

5. man _____

6. moose _____

7. person _____

8. deer _____

9. mouse _____

10. sheep _____

11. ox _____

12. fish _____

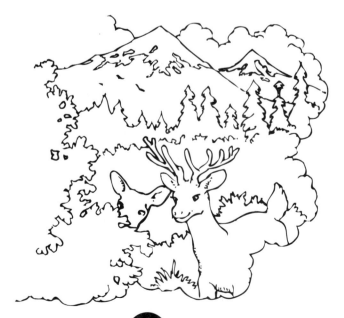

Name _____ Date _____

Half a Loaf

To make **plural nouns**:

Add *s* to most singular nouns ending in vowel-*o*.
> **Example:**   rodeo = rodeos

Add *es* to most singular nouns ending in consonant-*o*.
> **Example:**   tomato = tomatoes

Change the *f* to *v* and add *es* to singular nouns ending in *f*.
> **Example:**   leaf = leaves

Circle the correct plural form of each noun.

1. potato	potatoes	potatos	potato's
2. half	halfs	halves	halvs
3. mosquito	mosquitoes	mosquitoz	mosquitos
4. hero	heros	heroes	heros'
5. loaf	loaves	loafs	loafes
6. zero	zeroes	zeros	zeroz
7. calf	calfs	calves	calfz
8. volcano	volcanoes	volcanos	volcanoes'
9. shelf	shelfs	shelvs	shelves
10. hoof	hooves	hoofs	hoofes

28

0-7424-1803-0 *Building Grammar & Writing Skills*

Name _____ Date _____

Desert Treasures

To make a singular noun show **possession** or ownership, add an apostrophe and an *s*.

Examples: Deandre   *Deandre's* hiking shoes are muddy.
tree   The *tree's* limbs are heavy with snow.

Change each noun to its possessive form.

1. snake _____

2. rock _____

3. bird _____

4. lizard _____

5. sand _____

6. shrub _____

7. tortoise _____

Write a sentence using the possessive form of each word.

8. Kelly _____

9. truck _____

10. insect _____

11. rope _____

12. spider _____

0-7424-1803-0 *Building Grammar & Writing Skills*

Name _____ Date _____

Fast Food Fun

To make a plural noun ending in *s* show **possession** or ownership, add an apostrophe after the *s*.

    Examples: boys   The *boys'*mother took them to the skate park.

If the plural noun does not end in *s*, add an apostrophe and an *s*.

    Examples: men   The *men's* fitting room is on the left.

Change each plural noun to its possessive form.

    1. cups _____

    2. hamburgers _____

    3. french fries _____   **7.** parents _____

    4. workers _____   **8.** milkshakes _____

    5. straws _____   **9.** sundaes _____

    6. children _____   **10.** fish _____

Write a sentence using the possessive form of each plural noun.

    11. girls _____

    12. women _____

    13. hats _____

    14. snacks _____

    15. yo-yos _____

30

Name _____ Date _____

A Day at the Beach

A **verb** names an action or a state of being.

Examples: riding, playing, is, was

Look at the picture. Write 10 action verbs that could describe what is happening in the picture.

_____   _____

_____   _____

_____   _____

_____   _____

_____   _____

     0-7424-1803-0 *Building Grammar & Writing Skills*

Name _____ Date _____

Being Me

Most verbs name an action. The verb *be* is different. It tells about someone or something. *Am*, *is*, and *are* are forms of the verb *be*.

Use *is* with one person, place, or thing.

Example: Mr. Wu *is* my teacher.

Use *are* with more than one person, place or thing, or with the word *you*.

Examples: We *are* studying mummies.
                You *are* happy.

Use *am* with the word *I*.

Example: I *am* happy today.

Fill in each blank with the correct form of the verb *be* (*is, am* or *are*).

1. My house _____ brown.

2. My favorite color _____ blue.

3. We _____ baking cookies today.

4. I _____ going to the movies on Saturday.

5. My friends _____ going with me.

6. What _____ your phone number?

7. You _____ standing on my foot.

8. I _____ four feet tall.

9. The firefighter _____ driving the engine.

10. Charles and I _____ playing football.

11. The band _____ playing "The Star-Spangled Banner."

12. Denver _____ east of Los Angeles.

13. You _____ a nice person.

14. _____ I your best friend?

32

Name _____ Date _____

Helping Our Earth

Sometimes an action verb needs help from another verb called a **helping verb**.

Common Helping Verbs					
am	can	does	is	shall	will
are	could	had	may	should	would
be	did	has	might	was	
been	do	have	must	were	

Underline the action verb in each sentence. Then choose the best helping verb and write it on the line.

1. Jasmine's family _____ planning a recycling project.
   (is   had   are)

2. They _____ talking to their neighbors.
   (is   may   are)

3. Mr. Chavez _____ look for old newspapers and magazines.
   (will   do   were)

4. The Ong children _____ gathering bags to collect plastic bottles.
   (should   are   did)

5. Jasmine _____ open a lemonade stand to keep us cool.
   (have   was   might)

6. Mrs. Zanuto said she _____ drive us to the recycling center.
   (would   be   are)

7. We _____ respect our planet.
   (have   must   are)

33

   0-7424-1803-0 *Building Grammar & Writing Skills*

Name _____ Date _____

Rainy Day Fun

Present-tense verbs tell what is happening now.
Past-tense verbs tell what happened in the past.

To change most action verbs to past tense, add *ed*.

    jump to *jumped*

To change "being" verbs to past tense, follow these rules:

    am to *was*   *are* to *were*   *is* to *was*

Read each sentence. Underline the verb.
Then rewrite each sentence and change the verb to past tense.

1. It is raining.

_____

2. Justin and Kendra splash in puddles.

_____

3. Paola plays in the rain.

_____

4. Lynda bakes cookies for a snack.

_____

5. Pam and Arthur watch movies on television.

_____

6. Carlos and Keith are at the library.

_____

7. I dash to the barn.

_____

8. I am soaking wet.

_____

0-7424-1803-0 *Building Grammar & Writing Skills*

Name _____ Date _____

Trip to the Mall

Present-tense verbs tell what is happening now.
Past-tense verbs tell what happened in the past.

To change most action verbs to past tense, add *ed.*
   jump to *jumped*
Change verbs that end in *e* to past tense by adding *d.*
   race to *raced*
Change verbs that end in consonant-*y* to past tense
by changing the *y* to *i* and adding *ed.*
   try to *tried*
Change verbs that end with a vowel followed by a consonant
to past tense by doubling the consonant and adding *ed.*
   stop to *stopped*

Fill in each blank with the past tense of the verb.

   I was _____ to a birthday party. So my mom, my sister, and I _____ to
        (invite)   (hurry)

the mall to buy a gift. We _____ off the elevator. "Don't touch anything!" Mom
                                    (hop)

said. So, I _____ everything. I _____ the sweaters off the tables. I _____
              (touch)   (pull)   (try)

on all the hats. I _____ a game of hide-and-seek with my sister. She _____
                      (play)   (cry)

when I _____ her. I _____ her to make her feel better.
          (trip)   (hug)

   We _____ at a candy shop. I _____ my lips at the chewy bears. I
         (stop)   (lick)

_____ my mom to buy some. She _____. I _____ to get my friend
  (beg)   (refuse)   (decide)

chewy bears. I _____ as the salesperson _____ the gift. I _____
                  (smile)   (wrap)   (carry)

the candy out to the car. What do you think _____ to the gift?
                                                (happen)

35

Name _____ Date _____

Verb Matchup

Some **past-tense verbs** do not end in *ed*. Some verbs stay the same, some verbs change just a little, and some change to almost a completely different word.

    Examples: *fall* to *fell*   *think* to *thought*

Cut out all the word squares. Place each present-tense verb next to the correct past-tense verb. On a separate sheet of paper, write five sentences using the past-tense form of the verbs.

				begin	eat	put
	read	make	say	brought	began
bring	feel	find	know	cut	made
cut	grow	wrote	grew	ate	said
fly	leave	read	felt	knew	let
found	put	let	write	left	flew

    0-7424-1803-0 *Building Grammar & Writing Skills*

Name _____ Date _____

Shark Tank

A **pronoun** is a word that takes the place of a noun.

A **subject pronoun** takes the place of a noun in the subject of a sentence.

An **object pronoun** takes the place of a noun that follows a verb or a word such as *to, from, of, at, with,* or *by.*

		Subject Pronouns				
I	you	he	she	it	we	they

		Object Pronouns					
me	you	him	her	it	us	you	them

Replace each underlined word or phrase with a subject or object pronoun listed above. Rewrite each sentence correctly.

1. The <u>third-grade class</u> went on a class trip to the aquarium.

_____

2. <u>The aquarium</u> was filled with interesting sea life.

_____

3. Janice shrieked when <u>Janice</u> saw the shark tank.

_____

4. "<u>The sharks</u> have really sharp teeth," Janice said.

_____

5. David reassured Janice, "<u>The sharks</u> can't hurt Janice."

_____

6. <u>The third-grade class</u> believed David because <u>David</u> is the tour guide.

_____

37

0-7424-1803-0 *Building Grammar & Writing Skills*

Name _____ Date _____

In Possession

A **possessive pronoun** takes the place of a possessive noun.

    Examples: *Belinda's* bicycle is red.   *Shane* and *Bob's* cat is gray.

                 Her bicycle is red.   *Their* cat is gray.

Possessive Pronouns
my   your   her   his   its   our   their

Draw a line from each possessive noun to the correct possessive pronoun.

1. Leticia's   their

2. the boat's   our

3. the children's   their

4. the class'   his

5. my friends' and my   its

6. Matthew's   her

Write a sentence using each possessive pronoun in the box above.

7. _____

8. _____

9. _____

10. _____

11. _____

12. _____

13. _____

38

Name _____ Date _____

Describe It

Adjectives describe nouns. They tell how many, what kind, or which one.

Examples: *Seven* children   *Purple* flowers   *That* toy

Write three adjectives that describe each noun.

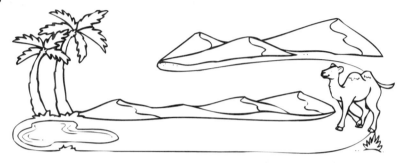

puppy	desert
_____	_____
_____	_____
_____	_____

storm	city
_____	_____
_____	_____
_____	_____

beetle	tulip
_____	_____
_____	_____
_____	_____

computer	snow
_____	_____
_____	_____
_____	_____

 0-7424-1803-0 *Building Grammar & Writing Skills*

Name _____ Date _____

Making Comparisons

Adjectives that compare two things usually end in *er*.
    Example: Ants are *smaller* than ladybugs.

Adjectives that compare three or more things usually end in *est*.
    Example: February is the *shortest* month of the year.

Underline the adjective that best completes in each sentence.

  1. Margery is the (stronger, strongest) girl in third grade.

  2. The blue sailboat is (faster, fastest) than the red sailboat.

  3. July is usually (hotter, hottest) than January.

  4. Which instrument is the (louder, loudest) one in the orchestra?

  5. Turtles are (slower, slowest) than rabbits.

  6. Tran is the (funnier, funniest) student in our class.

  7. Your slice of cake is (thicker, thickest) than mine.

  8. Frogs jump (higher, highest) than mice.

  9. Mount Everest is the (taller, tallest) mountain in the world.

10. The summer solstice is the (longer, longest) day of the year.

Use these adjectives to write four sentences that compare.

11. short   _____

12. bright _____

13. smart   _____

14. cold   _____

0-7424-1803-0 *Building Grammar & Writing Skills*

Name _____ Date _____

Adventurous Adverbs

Adverbs describe verbs. They usually tell how, when, and where an action happened.

Examples: The horse walked *slowly*.
We went riding *yesterday*.

Fill in each blank with an adverb from the Word Box.

Word Box				
slowly	carefully	yesterday	recklessly	nearby
there	softly	later	happily	beautifully

1. Sandy _____ ate her ice-cream cone.

2. Put your backpack _____.

3. Milo skated _____ and broke his wrist.

4. Tyler visited the museum _____.

5. When the baby is asleep, we must speak _____.

6. I have soccer practice _____.

7. The bear watched her cubs play _____.

8. Charlotte sings _____.

9. Mother decorated the cake _____.

10. The jellyfish swims _____.

0-7424-1803-0 *Building Grammar & Writing Skills*

Name _____ Date _____

Sports Articles

A, *an*, and *the* are special adjectives called **articles**.
A and *an* are used to introduce singular nouns. Use *a* when the next word begins with a consonant sound. Use *an* when the next word begins with a vowel sound.

Examples: *a* chair   *an* antelope

The is used to introduce both singular and plural nouns.

Examples: *the* beaver *the* flowers

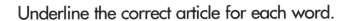

Underline the correct article for each word.

1. (the, an)   field
2. (a, an)   award
3. (an, the)   ball
4. (a, the)   wheels
5. (a, an)   inning
6. (an, the)   sticks
7. (the, a)   goalposts
8. (a, an)   obstacle
9. (a, an)   umpire
10. (an, the)   quarterback
11. (a, the)   outfield
12. (the, an)   surfboard
13. (an, the)   team
14. (an, the)   shin guards
15. (a, an)   helmet

16. (a, an)   glove
17. (the, an)   net
18. (a, the)   skates
19. (a, the)   tennis shoes
20. (a, an)   touchdown
21. (a, the)   ice
22. (a, an)   wave
23. (the, an)   skateboard
24. (a, the)   water
25. (the, a)   goggles
26. (an, the)   scoreboard
27. (a, the)   spectators
28. (the, an)   uneven bars
29. (a, the)   hurdles
30. (a, an)   time-out

   0-7424-1803-0 *Building Grammar & Writing Skills*

Name _____ Date _____

Put It All Together

Contractions are two words that are shortened and put together to make one word. An **apostrophe** is used in place of the missing letters.

    Examples: does not = doesn't
                       cannot = can't

Draw a line from each pair of words to its matching contraction.

  1. is not   weren't

  2. are not   wasn't

  3. was not   aren't

  4. were not   isn't

  5. have not   didn't

  6. can not   haven't

  7. do not   couldn't

  8. did not   can't

  9. could not   shouldn't

10. should not   don't

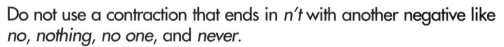

Do not use a contraction that ends in *n't* with another negative like *no, nothing, no one,* and *never.*

    Incorrect: I didn't get *no* milk.
    Correct: I didn't get *any* milk.

Rewrite each sentence correctly on the back of this paper.

11. Molly doesn't have no tennis shoes.

12. Brett can't never find his baseball glove.

13. We aren't doing nothing on Saturday.

14. Trent wouldn't never eat fried worms.

43

            0-7424-1803-0 *Building Grammar & Writing Skills*

Name _____ Date _____

A New Bicycle

The verb in a sentence must be the same tense as the subject.
This is called **subject–verb agreement.**

Present tense tells what is happening right now.
If the verb is present tense and the subject is singular, add an *s* or *es* to the verb.

Examples: The branch *sways* softly in the breeze.
Hannah *munches* on carrot sticks

If verb is present tense and the subject is plural, do not add an *s* or *es* to the verb.

Examples: Gophers *live* underground.
They *crush* plants.

Read each sentence. Underline the form of the verb that agrees with the subject.

1. Mary (receive, receives) a new bicycle on her birthday.

2. She (put, puts) on her helmet.

3. Tony and Jennifer (ride, rides) to Mary's house.

4. Mary (jump, jumps) on the shiny red bike.

5. She (spin, spins) around in the driveway.

6. The friends (laugh, laughs) as they ride.

7. They (race, races) down the sidewalk.

8. The streamers (fly, flies) in the wind.

9. Jennifer (reach, reaches) the finish line first.

10. Tony (finish, finishes) last.

11. Mary (enjoy, enjoys) her new bike.

12. They will all (meet, meets) tomorrow for another ride.

44

Name _____ Date _____

All About Giraffes

The **subject** of a sentence tells whom or what the sentence is about. It is a noun or pronoun. The subject can be one word or more than one word.

Examples:

> *Giraffes* eat leaves.
> Its *brown and beige coat* helps the giraffe blend into its surroundings.

Circle the subject in each sentence.

1. The giraffe is a mammal.

2. Its neck is very long and muscular.

3. Its long tongue is used to pull leaves from branches.

4. A giraffe can go without drinking water for more than a month.

5. Its large, solid hooves are used to kick predators.

6. Calves can stand up 20 minutes after they're born.

7. It can live up to 26 years.

8. An adult male leads a herd.

Complete each sentence by adding a subject.

9. _____ live in Africa.

10. _____ can see them at the zoo.

11. _____ are doing a report on giraffes.

12. _____ has seen giraffes at the animal park.

0-7424-1803-0 *Building Grammar & Writing Skills*

Name _____ Date _____

The Moon

The **predicate** is the part of the sentence that tells what the subject is or does. It can be one word or more than one word.

Examples: The moon *glows*.
The moon *orbits the Earth*.

Underline the predicate in each sentence.

1. Earth has one moon.

2. The moon revolves around the Earth.

3. One lunar month is approximately 30 days.

4. The diameter of the moon is approximately 2,160 miles.

5. Scientists study craters, mountain ranges, and plains on the surface of the moon.

6. Exploration of the moon began in the 1960s.

7. Astronauts collected rock samples from the moon.

8. Geologists study the rocks.

Complete each sentence by adding a predicate.

9. The moon _____

10. Astronauts _____

11. People on Earth _____

12. Space exploration _____

0-7424-1803-0 *Building Grammar & Writing Skills*

Name _____ Date _____

Match It!

The **subject** of a sentence tells whom or what the sentence is about. It is a noun or pronoun. The subject can be one word or more than one word.

The **predicate** is the part of the sentence that tells what the subject is or does. It can be one word or more than one word.

Write the letter of each predicate before the subject that completes the sentence.

Subjects

____ **1.** Parker

____ **2.** The ballerina

____ **3.** My sister's parakeet

____ **4.** Our teacher

____ **5.** The amusement park ride

____ **6.** That ice cream sundae

____ **7.** Emily

____ **8.** The goalie

Predicates

a. was closed for repairs.

b. dove into the freezing cold pool.

c. made the save.

d. assigned the class lots of homework.

e. likes to ride his skateboard.

f. flew out of the window.

g. twirled on her toes.

h. is almost to sweet to eat!

47

Name _____ Date _____

Pizza Pie

A **sentence** is a group of words that expresses a complete thought.
It contains a subject and a predicate.

Example: Miranda eats pizza every day.

A **fragment** does not express a complete thought. It might be missing either the subject or the predicate.

Example: Pepperoni and cheese on it

Read each group of words. Decide if it is a sentence or fragment.
Circle **S** if it is a sentence. Circle **F** if it is a fragment.

1.	Pizza tastes delicious.	S	F
2.	Let the dough rise before spreading it out.	S	F
3.	Dough in the air	S	F
4.	Anthony pours tomato sauce on the crust.	S	F
5.	Mom arranges the toppings on the sauce.	S	F
6.	Mario sprinkles the pizza with red pepper.	S	F
7.	More cheese	S	F
8.	We bake the pizza in the oven for 10 minutes.	S	F
9.	Served hot and bubbly	S	F
10.	Cut slices	S	F

Write five sentences of your own about pizza. Each sentence needs a subject and a predicate.

11. _____

12. _____

13. _____

14. _____

15. _____

48

0-7424-1803-0 *Building Grammar & Writing Skills*

Name _____ Date _____

Fun at the Park

A **compound sentence** combines two simple sentences with ideas that go together. The ideas are joined together by conjunctions such as *or*, *but*, or *and*. Use a comma before the conjunction.

Simple Sentence: Michael drives a go-cart.
Compound Sentence: Michael drives a go-cart, and Phillip rides a bike.

Combine the simple sentences to make a compound sentence.
Use a comma and *or*, *but*, or *and*.

1. Sheila wears roller skates. Andy rides a skateboard.

_____

2. The children play in the park. The adults watch.

_____

3. Seth buys ice cream. Karen prefers hot dogs.

_____

4. Fishing is fun. It is not allowed in this pond.

_____

5. My mom flies a kite. My dad unpacks the lunch basket.

_____

6. You can eat potato chips. You can eat tortilla chips.

_____

0-7424-1803-0 *Building Grammar & Writing Skills*

Name _____ Date _____

Katelyn's Garden

A **run-on sentence** is two or more sentences that run together.
Use punctuation and capitalization to make better sentences.

Run-on: Katelyn's garden is in the backyard she works there on each day.
Correct: Katelyn's garden is in the backyard. She works there each day.

Rewrite each run-on sentence correctly. Write two shorter sentences, or
connect the ideas with a conjunction.

1. Katelyn cleared the garden she raked the leaves and collected rocks.

_____

2. Katelyn planted seeds she planted beans and pumpkins.

_____

3. The seeds grow quickly they like warm sunshine.

_____

4. Water helps the plants grow Katelyn waters them every day.

_____

5. Insects visit Katelyn's garden some bugs are good.

_____

6. Pulling weeds is not very fun it is an important job.

_____

7. Pumpkins grow very large beans grow very tall.

_____

_____

8. Katelyn harvests the vegetables they taste good.

_____

_____

0-7424-1803-0 *Building Grammar & Writing Skills*

Name _____ Date _____

My Dog

A **paragraph** is a group of sentences that tell about one main idea. It begins with a **topic sentence**. **Supporting sentences** tell more about the topic. The paragraph ends with a **concluding sentence**.

Topic Sentence:	Main idea
Supporting Sentence:	Give more detail about he main idea
Concluding Sentence:	Rephrases the topic sentence; summerizes the main idea

Underline the topic sentence in this paragraph. Number each of the supporting sentences. Circle the concluding sentence.

My dog is the smartest dog in the world. ☐ Her name is Lulu. ☐ She

can fetch the newspaper when Dad asks her to. ☐ When Mom is sad,

Lulu cheers her up by licking her face. ☐ I really like it when Lulu

helps me find my lost tennis shoe. Lulu is the best dog!

On the back of this paper, write your own paragraph about a pet you have or would like to have.

0-7424-1803-0 *Building Grammar & Writing Skills*

Name _____ Date _____

Tip-Top Topics

A **paragraph** is a group of sentences that tell about one main idea.
It begins with a topic sentence. The **topic sentence** is the main idea of the
paragraph. The rest of the paragraph relates to the idea given in the topic
sentence. It is usually the first sentence in the paragraph.

Write a topic sentence for each paragraph.

_____. First, I put on
my helmet. Next, I practiced balancing on the bike. My mom gave me a little push,
and I was on my way. I pedaled as fast as I could. I steered carefully. I was riding
by myself!

_____. We go outside
and eat our snacks. When the teacher excuses
us, we race out to the field. Some kids play on
the jungle gym and others swing on the swing
set. A game of soccer is organized. Everyone
has fun at recess.

_____. We use
computers to help us write reports. We use them to surf the web and learn new
things. Computers ring up our purchases at the store. They can even make phone
calls for us. Computers are a wonderful invention.

_____. He spills milk
on the table at snack time. He talks when the teacher is talking and gets sent to the
principal's office. He fools around in line for the bus. Bradley Johnson is always
in trouble.

0-7424-1803-0 *Building Grammar & Writing Skills*

Name _____ Date _____

Support System

A **paragraph** is a group of sentences that tell about one main idea.
The **topic sentence** tells the main idea of the paragraph.
The **supporting sentences** tell more about the main idea.

Write three supporting sentences for each topic sentence.

Police officers are very helpful.

_____

_____

_____

I was really scared during the thunderstorm.

_____

_____

_____

My favorite amusement park ride is the bumper cars.

_____

_____

_____

Saturday is the best day of the week.

_____

_____

_____

Name _____ Date _____

In Conclusion . . .

A **paragraph** is a group of sentences that tell about one main idea.
The **topic sentence** tells the main idea of the paragraph.
The **supporting sentences** tell more about the main idea.
The **concluding sentence** rephrases the main idea or connects
to the next paragraph.

Write a concluding sentence for each paragraph.

It looks like rain. Heavy gray clouds are collecting in the sky. The icy wind
is blowing through my sweater. Drops splatter the sidewalk and my glasses.

_____

_____

The flowers bloom in brilliant colors. Daffodils smile with their yellow faces.
Purple irises complement the pink tulips. Many people cut the white daisies to
put in vases.

_____

_____

 Birds build nests to prepare a home for their eggs.
First, they find a safe place for a nest. Then, they
collect twigs, branches, and leaves. Finally, the birds
arrange the nest.

_____

_____

54

0-7424-1803-0 *Building Grammar & Writing Skills*

Name _____ Date _____

Write Your Own Paragraph

My Topic: _____

Topic Sentence

_____

_____

Supporting Sentence 1

_____

_____

Supporting Sentence 2

_____

_____

Supporting Sentence 3

_____

_____

Concluding Sentence

_____

_____

Now, rewrite your paragraph on a separate sheet of paper. Remember to indent the first line.

© McGraw-Hill Children's Publishing

0-7424-1803-0 *Building Grammar & Writing Skills*

Name _____ Date _____

The Princess

Adjectives are describing words. They tell how many, what kind, or which one. When you use adjectives in your writing, it makes the sentences clearer and more interesting.

Example: The car speeds away.   The sleek, red car speeds away.

Read the story below.

Once upon a time, there was a princess who wore a hat. She lived in a castle with her cat. The princess was bored. "There is nothing to do," the princess complained. She wandered off into the garden in search of adventure. "What is this I see?" she cried. There was a box next to a tree. The princess opened the lid to find a cloak. "This is a cloak!" she exclaimed. But when she slipped it on, the princess vanished!

Use words from the Word Box or your own words to make the story more interesting.

Word Box								
beautiful	magical	pointy	fat	cruel	huge	wonderful	silly	fantastic
fun	blue	cold	funny	exciting	shy	knotty	rusty	strong	tiny	sweet

Once upon a time, there was a _____ princess who wore a

_____ hat. She lived in a _____ castle with her

_____ cat. The princess was bored. "There is nothing to do," the

_____ princess complained. She wandered off into the

_____ garden in search of adventure. "What is this I see?" she

cried. There was a _____ box next to a _____ tree.

The princess opened the lid to find a _____ cloak. "This is a

_____ cloak!" she exclaimed. But when she slipped it on, the

_____ princess vanished!

0-7424-1803-0 *Building Grammar & Writing Skills*

Name _____ Date _____

Exciting Words

Adjectives are describing words. They tell how many, what kind, or which one. When you use adjectives in your writing, it makes the sentences clearer and more interesting. Some adjectives are used more than others and get boring or don't describe something very well. Try to use more interesting adjectives when describing a person, place, or thing.

Good: The ball bounced away.
Better: The bright, red ball bounced away.

Change each adjective to make the phrase more interesting.

1. nice girl   _____ girl

2. pretty flower   _____ flower

3. good dog   _____ dog

4. tall man   _____ man

5. happy boy   _____ boy

6. big truck   _____ truck

7. small box   _____ box

8. bad smell   _____ smell

9. many animals   _____ animals

10. fun ride   _____ ride

0-7424-1803-0 *Building Grammar & Writing Skills*

Name _____ Date _____

Seashore Fun

Verbs are action words. They tell what is happening in the sentences. Some verbs are boring and used too often. You can make your writing clearer and more exciting by changing some verbs.

Example: Barbara *put* peanut butter on her bread.
Barbara *slathered* peanut butter on her bread.

Change the underlined word in each sentence. Use the verbs in the Word Box to make the sentences more exciting.

Word Box				
thundered	streaked	explained	scurried	splashed
danced	grumbled	pitched	cried	hopped
steered	gathered	rescued	sailed	shrieked

_____ **1.** Dad <u>drove</u> the car toward the beach.

_____ **2.** The seagulls <u>played</u> at the edge of the water.

_____ **3.** Waves <u>broke</u> on the sand.

_____ **4.** Tomas <u>found</u> seashells at the seashore.

_____ **5.** "What's that?" Petra <u>said</u>.

_____ **6.** "It's a sand crab," Bobby <u>said</u>.

_____ **7.** The sand crabs <u>went</u> away when he lifted the rock.

_____ **8.** Sam <u>ran</u> across the hot sand.

_____ **9.** Jessica <u>swam</u> in the surf.

_____ **10.** The beach ball <u>went</u> through the air.

On the back of this paper, write five sentences of your own about a day at the beach. Use words from the Word Box.

58

Name _____ Date _____

The Five Senses

When you are writing, you can use your five senses to help you describe something.
Think about what the reader might see, hear, smell, taste, and feel.
Use words that relate to those senses.

See: shiny, round

Hear: squeaky, roaring

Smell: rotten, smoky

Taste: spicy, sweet

Feel: sharp, prickly

Write two describing words for each noun. Use your five senses to help you.

1. strawberry   _____   _____

2. pony   _____   _____

3. sand   _____   _____

4. leather coat   _____   _____

5. golf ball   _____   _____

6. bicycle chain   _____   _____

7. paper   _____   _____

8. milk   _____   _____

Now, use two of the above nouns and describing words to write a descriptive sentence.

_____

   0-7424-1803-0 *Building Grammar & Writing Skills*

Name _____ Date _____

Let's Golf!

By staying on the topic when you are writing, you will help the reader stay focused on what you are trying to say. Any extra information should be removed. This will help your reader follow your ideas.

Read the following paragraph. Cross out two sentences that do not help the reader focus on the topic.

Golf is a popular sport. Millions of people all over the world enjoy golf. Golf originated more than 500 years ago. People play golf in the United States, Australia, Japan, and South Africa. There are more than 14,000 golf courses in the United States alone! Mary, Queen of Scots, played golf a long time ago. People can watch professional golfers play on television. It is a sport that men, women, and children can play.

Rewrite the paragraph correctly.

_____

_____

_____

_____

_____

_____

_____

_____

0-7424-1803-0 *Building Grammar & Writing Skills*

Name _____ Date _____

Careers

Grouping your ideas helps keep your writing focused and organized. It helps the reader follow what you are saying.

Read the sentences and phrases below. Choose one topic sentence and write it on the line. Then list the supporting facts.

Example: **Topic sentence:** <u>Teachers are important people.</u>
Supporting fact: <u>show students how to read</u>
Supporting fact: <u>teach students how to do math</u>
Supporting fact: <u>help children learn to be good people</u>

Doctors help people get better.
use new ingredients
look into your mouth with a tongue depressor
put out fires in homes
rescue people who are in trouble
Chefs have a very fun job.
give you medicine
taste all the delicious pastries
Firefighters are heroes.
create lots of interesting meals
check your ears
take people to the hospital when they are sick
make food in a big kitchen
listen to your chest with a stethoscope

Topic sentence: _____

Supporting fact: _____

Supporting fact: _____

Supporting fact: _____

0-7424-1803-0 *Building Grammar & Writing Skills*

Name _____ Date _____

Using a Dictionary

A **dictionary** can help you find the meaning and spelling of words. To use a dictionary, all you need to know is the alphabet!

All words in a dictionary are listed in alphabetical order. The words in **bold** are called **entry words**.

At the top of each page in a dictionary there are **guide words**. The first guide word is the first word found on that page. The second guide word is the last word found on that page. The other words on the page will appear in alphabetical order between those two guide words.

gill (gil) *noun* 1. The organ for breathing in most animals that live in water

girl (gurl) *noun* 1. A female child

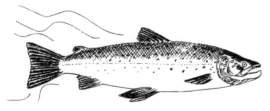

The **phonetic spelling** of each word appears in parentheses next to the entry word. The **part of speech** is usually in italics and appears after the phonetic spelling. It may sometimes be abbreviated (*noun = n. verb = v. adjective = adj. adverb = adv.*).

1. Would you find the word *gumball* on this page? _____

2. Would you find the word *ginger* on this page? _____

3. What part of speech is the word *gill*? _____

4. Write the definition for *girl*. _____

62

Name _____ Date _____

Using a Thesaurus

A **thesaurus** can help you find synonyms and antonyms of words.

All words in a thesaurus are listed in alphabetical order.
The words in **bold** are called **entry words**.

At the top of each page in a thesaurus there are guide words. The first guide word is the first word found on that page. The second guide word is the last word found on that page. The other words on the page will appear in alphabetical order between those two guide words.

fair (*syn*) pale, sunny, just, honest, equitable
(*ant*) fraudulent, unfair, foul

fame (*syn*) distinction, glory, reputation, notoriety
(*ant*) annonymity, disrepute, infamy

Use a thesaurus to find a synonym for each word below.

1. tell _____

2. friend _____

3. fix _____

4. pretty _____

5. good _____

6. fast _____

7. run _____

8. easy _____

9. job _____

10. yell _____

Name _____ Date _____

Organize a Web

Choose a topic and write it in the center circle. Then complete the web by writing a supporting detail in each oval.

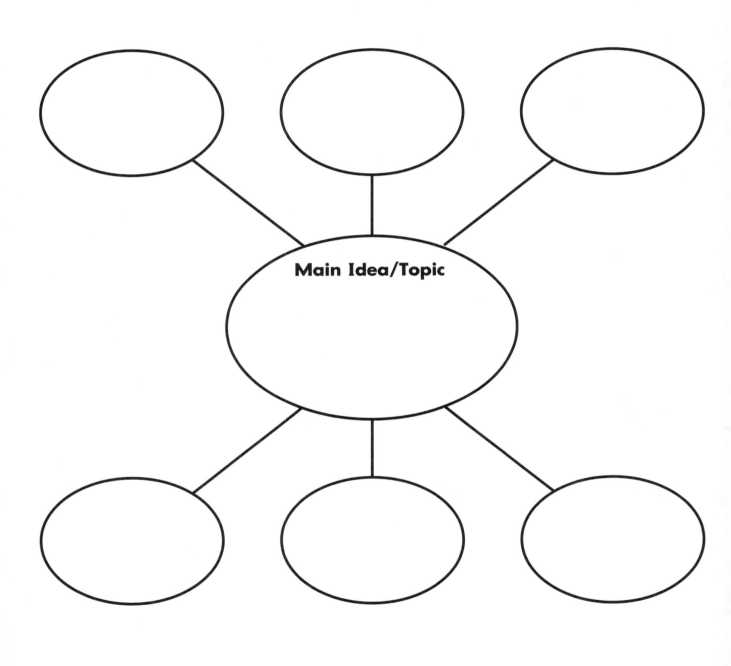

0-7424-1803-0 *Building Grammar & Writing Skills*

Name _____ Date _____

Organize a Chart

Complete this chart for your topic.

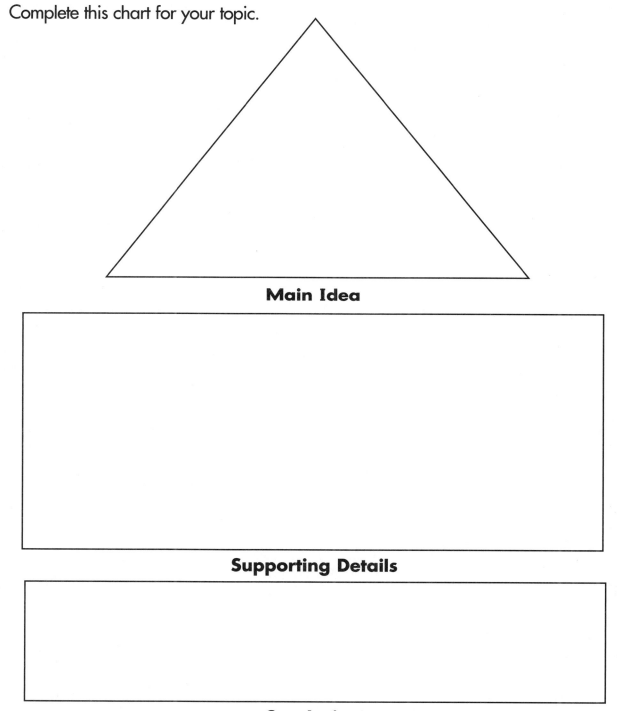

Main Idea

Supporting Details

Conclusion

0-7424-1803-0 *Building Grammar & Writing Skills*

Name _____ Date _____

Organize a Diagram

Complete this diagram for your topic.

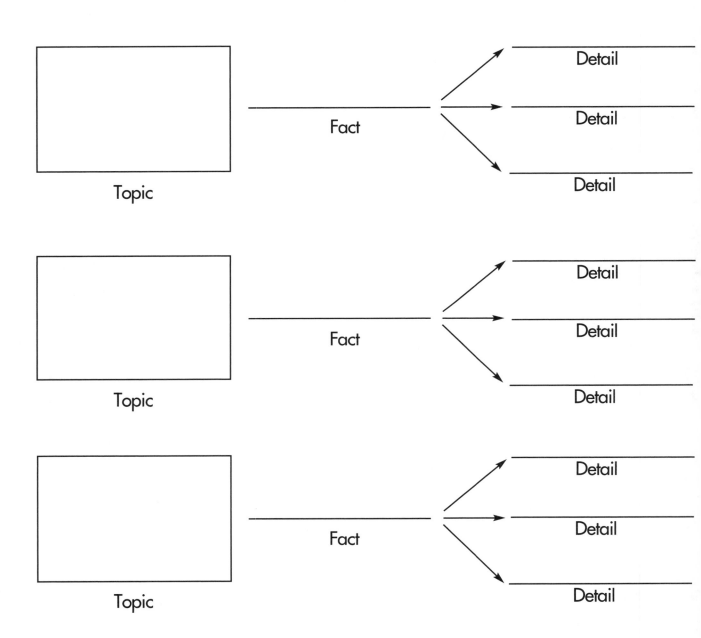

0-7424-1803-0 *Building Grammar & Writing Skills*

Name _____ Date _____

Organize an Outline

Complete this outline for your topic.

Topic: _____

I. Main Idea: _____

  A. Subtopic _____

    1. Supporting Detail: _____

    2. Supporting Detail: _____

  B. Subtopic _____

    1. Supporting Detail: _____

    2. Supporting Detail: _____

II. Main Idea: _____

  A. Subtopic _____

    1. Supporting Detail: _____

    2. Supporting Detail: _____

  B. Subtopic _____

    1. Supporting Detail: _____

    2. Supporting Detail: _____

III. Main Idea: _____

  A. Subtopic _____

    1. Supporting Detail: _____

    2. Supporting Detail: _____

  B. Subtopic _____

    1. Supporting Detail: _____

    2. Supporting Detail: _____

 0-7424-1803-0 *Building Grammar & Writing Skills*

Name _____ Date _____

Sequencing Sentences

Stories and paragraphs have a beginning, middle, and end. When you are writing, make sure your sentences flow in a logical order.

Fill in the sequencing chart below for your topic. Number the boxes 1–4, according to what happens first, second, next and last.

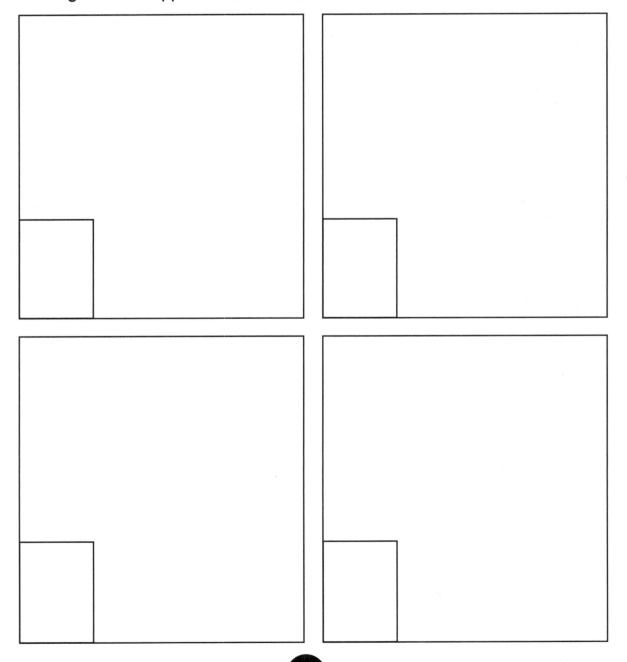

    0-7424-1803-0 *Building Grammar & Writing Skills*

Name _____ Date _____

Proofreading

Proofreading marks help us to revise our writing. These marks show where changes should be made.

⊩   Indent a paragraph

∧   Insert something

⤶   Take something out

m̲   Capitalize

Ɱ   Make lowercase

Edit the following paragraph. Use the proofreading marks above.

Margaret Thatcher was the First female prime minister in Great Britain.
A prime minister is like a president. Mrs. Thatcher was born in a town called
grantham in 1925. She went to school at the University of oxford. She became
chemist Later, she married a man named denis. After passing the bar
examination, She became a tax lawyer. Mrs. Thatcher got involved in politics
in 1959. She became the prime minister of Great Britain in 1979

Write your own paragraph on the back of this paper. Put in lots of mistakes
on purpose. Have a classmate use proofreading marks to edit your work.

0-7424-1803-0 *Building Grammar & Writing Skills*

Name _____ Date _____

Capitals in the Capitol

When you are reviewing your own or another student's writing, it helps to use proofreading marks to show where corrections are needed.

To show where a capital letter should be, write three short lines below the letter that needs to be capitalized.

Example: the mosleys took a trip to maryland.

Read the paragraph below. Write three short lines under letters that should be capitalized.

the white house was the first official building in washington, d.c. construction began on october 13, 1792. it is located at 1600 pennsylvania avenue in washington, d.c. it is the home of the president of the united states. the president and his family live in one section of the house. every american president except george washington has lived in the white house. the other section is used for the president's office. the white house is a beautiful building.

Name _____ Date _____

Perfect Punctuation

When you are reviewing your own or another student's writing, it helps to use proofreading marks to show where corrections are needed. Show where a punctuation mark is needed by using an insert mark (∧).

Example: Mary Jo Patty and Serena splashed in the lake

Insert punctuation marks where they are needed.

"A picnic at the lake is a wonderful idea" exclaimed Mary Jo "I will bring

cherry pie ham sandwiches and potato chips"

Patty replied, "Great I will bring a blanket umbrella and lemonade"

"Can I come" Serena asked "I could bring toys and games"

"Sure you can come" Patty said "We'll have lots of fun"

> 1543 Treetop Lane
>
> Forrester Illinois 56284
>
> July 23 2002
>
> Dear Mary Jo
>
>   Thank you for inviting me to the picnic at the lake It was really
>
> fun I enjoyed splashing in the lake and riding in the boat Your
>
> ham sandwiches tasted terrific I hope we can go to the lake again
>
>   Your friend
>
>   Serena

71

Name _____ Date _____

Home-Run Birthday Party

Adding detail makes writing clear and interesting. When you are reviewing your own or another student's writing, use an insert mark (∧) to add words.

Example: The bright, green, spiral notebook

Add details to this paragraph. For each suggestion, write an insert mark and write your suggestion above it.

The party was fun. We played games. We ate cake. Timmy opened his presents. He was happy to get a new baseball glove. Timmy's mom gave everyone a bag full of goodies before we went home. I had a great time at Timmy's party.

After you have added details to the paragraph, rewrite it below.

_____

_____

_____

_____

_____

_____

0-7424-1803-0 *Building Grammar & Writing Skills*

Name _____ Date _____

All About Birds

When you are reviewing your own or another student's writing, it helps to use proofreading marks to show where corrections are needed. Use this symbol (¶) to show where a new paragraph should begin.

A paragraph is a group of sentences that tell about one main idea. It begins with a topic sentence. Supporting sentences tell more about the topic. The paragraph ends with a concluding sentence.

Insert a proofreading mark (¶) where three different paragraphs begin in the report below.

Birds are unique animals. They can fly, except ostrich and kiwis. Birds hatch out of eggs, and many are born without feathers. Birds have bills instead of mouths, but they do not have teeth. They can cool their bodies while flying through the air or panting at rest. These features make birds special animals. There are different kinds of birds. Ostrich are the largest birds. They can be almost eight feet tall. Bee hummingbirds are the smallest birds and are no more than $2\frac{1}{2}$ inches tall. Hummingbirds are the only birds that are capable of flying backward. Penguins use their wings as oars when swimming through water. Woodpeckers drum on trees to create nesting holes and to communicate with other woodpeckers. Bird feathers have many different uses. The bright colors can attract mates or scare other birds. Feathers can act as camouflage to protect birds. They help protect birds from cold weather. They are water-repellent on swimming birds. Feathers are important to birds' survival.

0-7424-1803-0 *Building Grammar & Writing Skills*

Name _____ Date _____

Editing Checklists

Use these checklists when editing your own or someone else's writing.

Mechanics Checklist   Name _____

_____ Every sentence begins with a capital letter and ends
with the correct punctuation mark.

_____ Commas are in the right places.

_____ Words that need capital letters begin with capital letters.

_____ All words are spelled correctly.

_____ All sentences are one complete thought.

_____ There are no fragments or run-ons.

_____ The beginning of each paragraph is indented.

Checked by _____

Style Checklist   Name _____

_____ Verbs are interesting and exciting.

_____ Adjectives describe with detail. No boring words are used.

_____ Sentences show, not tell.

_____ Story has a beginning, a middle, and an end.

_____ Paragraphs have a topic sentence, supporting sentences,
and a concluding sentence.

_____ Each sentence does not begin with the same word.

Checked by _____

74

Name _____ Date _____

Publish Your Writing

You can publish your writing in many different ways—not just pencil and paper!

Make a book jacket.

Paint a mural.

Create a magazine.

Write an encyclopedia article.

Have a read-around.

Make a banner.

Post a bulletin board.

Add graphics.

Make a videotape.

Make a game or puzzle.

Laminate your writing.

Print a poster.

Keep a portfolio.

Make a picture book.

Make a diorama.

Make a comic strip.

Invite parents for story time.

Make a puppet show.

Imagine skywriting.

Sew it into a quilt or pillow.

Write a letter to a relative.

Make a cube.

Make a toy with instructions.

Create a billboard.

Design a computer game.

Write a message in a bottle.

Make a class newsletter.

Host a poetry reading.

Create a newspaper.

Write a historical journal.

Draw a picture with words.

Frame your essay.

Hang a mobile.

Illustrate your writing.

Make a web site.

Record a CD.

Bind it into a book.

Make a collage.

Write on wallpaper and hang it.

Read it to a small child.

Write it on a T-shirt.

Act out the story.

Write a screenplay.

Write a song and sing it.

Design a bumper sticker.

Make a chain.

Tell a friend.

Read it to your teacher.

Put it in a time capsule.

Create a postcard.

Write a review.

Host a mystery writing party.

Write a will.

Read it on the public address system at school.

Write a letter to the principal, a pen pal, your parent, or the president.

0-7424-1803-0 *Building Grammar & Writing Skills*

Name _____ Date _____

Parts of a Friendly Letter

123 Main Street
Plainsville, NY 41698
January 30, 2002

Dear Frank,
   Our class just went on a field trip to
the aviation museum. I know how
much you like airplanes, so it reminded
me of you. I saw an open cockpit
biplane like the ones used in World
War I. Wouldn't it be cool to ride in
one of those?
   I hope you are having fun in school.
Does your class take any field trips?

                    Your friend,
                    Jack

Heading:
This can be your address and
the date, or just the date. It starts
halfway across the page.

Greeting:
It is the opening of the letter. It
usually starts with *Dear,* then the
person's name and a comma. It
starts on the left side of the page.

Body:
This is the main part of the
letter. Each paragraph has its
own main idea. Each new
paragraph is indented.

Closing:
It is the ending of the letter. It
usually says good-bye with
phrases like *Your friend, Your
grandson,* or *Love.* The first letter
in the first word is capitalized
and a comma follows the phrase.
It starts halfway across the page,
like the heading.

Signature:
Write your name. It goes below
the closing.

Write a letter to a friend or relative.
Make sure to include all the parts
of a friendly letter.

0-7424-1803-0 *Building Grammar & Writing Skills*

Name _____ Date _____

Dear Friend...

Use this form to write a letter to a friend or relative.

Heading   _____

_____

_____

_____ Greeting

_____

_____

_____

_____ Body

_____

_____

_____

Closing   _____

Signature   _____

    0-7424-1803-0 *Building Grammar & Writing Skills*

Name _____ Date _____

Writing Letters

There are many reasons to write a friendly letter. You might want to share some news with a friend or invite someone to a party. You might want to send someone a get-well note or thank someone for a gift.

Each letter has the same five parts, even if the purpose is different.

Invitation: Tell the reader when (date, time), where (location), and what kind of event it is (party, practice, meeting, etc.).

Thank-you Note: Tell the reader what you are thankful for, why you are thankful, and how much you appreciate the gift.

Get-well Note: Tell the reader you hope he or she is feeling well again soon, and try to cheer up the person with kind words.

Choose one kind of friendly letter. Write a letter to a friend or relative.

Heading _____

_____

_____

Greeting

_____

_____

_____

_____

_____

Body

_____

_____

Closing _____

Signature _____

0-7424-1803-0 *Building Grammar & Writing Skills*

Name _____ Date _____

Expository Paragraphs

An **expository paragraph** gives information about, describes, or explains something. There are many types of expository paragraphs:

An **informative paragraph** gives factual information about a topic.
A **descriptive paragraph** gives a description of a topic.
A **"how-to" paragraph** gives instructions on how to do something.
A **persuasive paragraph** tries to convince someone of something.

Read each paragraph below. Decide which kind of paragraph it is, and write it on the line.

I think it is time I had a new bicycle. My old bike has a flat tire. The paint is peeling off in long sheets. The rusty chain could cause me to fall off the bike and hurt myself. Can I get a new bike?

_____

Do you know how to make pudding? First, pour the milk into a bowl. Next, open the packet of pudding mix. Then, pour it into the bowl. Stir the milk and the dry mix until it starts to get firm. Finally, put the bowl in the refrigerator to chill.

_____

I love to eat ice cream. The smell of baking waffle cones and rich ice cream makes my mouth water. My eyes dance at the sight of the brilliant rows of ice cream choices. The cold shock of the first bite on my tongue is a sweet treat. The ice cream parlor is my favorite place!

_____

A butterfly is a special insect. It has four stages of life. A butterfly begins as an egg. Then, it changes into a caterpillar. The caterpillar spins a cocoon around itself while it changes form. Finally, the caterpillar comes out as a butterfly.

_____

0-7424-1803-0 *Building Grammar & Writing Skills*

Name _____ Date _____

A Horse, of Course!

An **informative paragraph** gives information about a topic.

Read these notes about horses. Fill in the organizer below with the information.
Rewrite your paragraph on a separate sheet of paper.

Horses are measured in hands—the width of a human hand—from the ground to the withers (the highest part of the back).

Arabian horses are about 15 hands high.

Shetland ponies are sometimes only 10 hands high.

Large horses, like the Belgian, can be more than 17 hands high.

Topic Sentence: _____

Fact 1: _____

Fact 2: _____

Fact 3: _____

Concluding Sentence: _____

_____

0-7424-1803-0 *Building Grammar & Writing Skills*

Name _____ Date _____

Best Friends

A **descriptive paragraph** gives a description of a topic. It helps the reader "see" what you are writing about.

Adjectives, sense words, and vivid verbs help your reader "see" what you are trying to describe.

Who is your best friend? List words that describe your best friend, and then draw them below.

On the back of this paper, write the first draft of a paragraph describing your best friend. Use some of the words you listed above. Then exchange paragraphs with a classmate. Circle any words in your partner's paragraph that do not help the reader "see" what is being described. Finally, replace the circled words in your own paragraph with more interesting words.

Name _____ Date _____

Revising the First Draft

Use descriptive words and vivid verbs to help your writing come alive! It helps the reader "see" what you are trying to say.

Read the first draft of this paragraph. What can you change to make this descriptive paragraph more interesting? Circle the words you want to change.

    Carly is my best friend. She is very nice. She is very pretty. Carly has blond hair and brown eyes. She wears her hair in a long braid. I like her because we always have fun together. I have known Carly for a long time.

Rewrite this paragraph using descriptive words and vivid verbs to help the reader "see" Carly.

_____

_____

_____

_____

_____

_____

_____

_____

_____

_____

PAPER

 0-7424-1803-0 *Building Grammar & Writing Skills*

Name _____ Date _____

Final Draft

Write a paragraph describing your best friend on a separate sheet of paper. Ask a friend to edit your work. Then write your final draft below. Draw a picture of your best friend in the frame.

_____

_____

_____

_____

_____

_____

_____

_____

_____

_____

_____

_____

0-7424-1803-0 *Building Grammar & Writing Skills*

Name _____ Date _____

Hula Hoop Fun

A "how-to" paragraph gives instructions to the reader about how to do something. The paragraph should give step-by-step instructions.

Number the following sentences in order as they should appear in a "how-to" paragraph.

How to Turn a Hula Hoop

_____ Let go of the hoop.

_____ Bring the hoop up around your waist.

_____ Twist the hoop.

_____ Keep swiveling your hips.

_____ Hold the hoop in both hands.

_____ Swivel your hips.

_____ Step into the hula hoop.

Now, write the paragraph telling the reader how to turn a hula hoop. Add your own topic sentence and concluding sentence. Add details to make your instructions more interesting to the reader.

_____

_____

_____

_____

_____

_____

_____

Name _____ Date _____

No School?

A **persuasive paragraph** attempts to convince someone of something. It usually gives the pros and the cons of the situation, and tries to convince the reader to accept or agree with the author's opinion. The writer must use reasons to support his or her position.

List some reasons why students should and should <u>not</u> go to school on Fridays.

Should students go to school on Fridays?

Pros (Yes)	Cons (No)
_____	_____
_____	_____
_____	_____
_____	_____
_____	_____
_____	_____

What do you think? Should students go to school on Fridays? On the back of this paper write a paragraph trying to convince your principal to agree with your opinion. Give at least three reasons to support your opinion.

0-7424-1803-0 *Building Grammar & Writing Skills*

Name _____ Date _____

Old Glory

It's sometimes difficult to tell the difference between a fact and an opinion.
A **fact** is something that is true and can be proven.
An **opinion** is something that a person feels or believes.

Write **F** next to each fact. Write **O** next to each opinion.

_____ **1.** The American flag is red, white, and blue.

_____ **2.** There are 13 stripes on the flag.

_____ **3.** Betsy Ross is the best seamstress in history.

_____ **4.** The 50 stars represent the 50 states in the United States.

_____ **5.** Red is the best color.

_____ **6.** Our school displays an American flag.

_____ **7.** Everyone should have an American flag at home.

_____ **8.** "The Star-Spangled Banner" is our national anthem.

_____ **9.** Whitney Houston sings the national anthem better than anyone.

_____ **10.** The national anthem is sung before all professional sporting events.

_____ **11.** "Old Glory" is a good name for the American flag.

_____ **12.** The American flag is a symbol of liberty.

0-7424-1803-0 *Building Grammar & Writing Skills*

Name _____ Date _____

The Five Ws

Informative writing should contain the five Ws: *who, what, where, when,* and *why.*

Find a newspaper or magazine article. While you are reading the article, look for each of the following:

Where did it happen?

Why is this important?

When did it happen?

Who was involved?

What happened?

0-7424-1803-0 *Building Grammar & Writing Skills*

Name _____ Date _____

Carpool

A **narrative** tells a story. Every story has a beginning, a middle, and an end.
The **beginning** introduces the characters and setting. The **middle** tells about the
problem and events. The **end** solves the problem and closes the story.

Draw a line from each story element to the correct part of the story.

Beginning: Introduces the
characters and the setting

Middle: Tells about the
problem and events

End: Solves the problem
and closes the story

She hauled the jack and
spare tire out of the back and
changed the tire. We were
soon back on the road and
made it to school just in time
for the bell.

Early Monday morning,
Mom was driving the carpool
to school. The three of us were
sitting in the back of the van.

All of a sudden, thump! Mom
quickly swerved off to the side
of the road. Jumping out, she
discovered a flat tire.

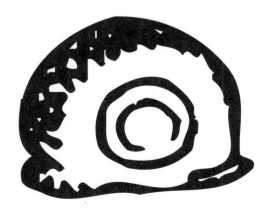

Name _____ Date _____

Story Organizer

A **narrative** tells a story. Every story has a beginning, a middle, and an end. The **beginning** introduces the characters and setting. The **middle** tells about the problem and events. The **end** solves the problem and closes the story.

Use the boxes below to help you organize a story you would like to write.

Beginning

• Who are the characters in your story?

_____

_____

• Where does the story take place?

_____

_____

_____

• When does the story happen?

_____

_____

_____

Middle

• What problem does the main character face?

_____

_____

• What events happen in the story to tell the reader about the problem?

_____

_____

_____

End

• How does the problem get solved?

_____

_____

• How does the story end?

_____

_____

_____

© McGraw-Hill Children's Publishing

0-7424-1803-0 *Building Grammar & Writing Skills*

Name _____ Date _____

Puzzle Planner

Use the pieces of the puzzle to help you plan your story.

Characters

Setting

Idea

Problem

Climax

Solution

Ending

0-7424-1803-0 *Building Grammar & Writing Skills*

Name _____ Date _____

Colorful Characters

The **characters** in a story can be real or imaginary. They can be people, animals, or things. The reader needs to know what the characters look like, what they think, and how they act.

Draw a line from each character name to the actions, words, or traits that best describe him or her.

1. Nagging Nellie

Has long shiny hair, big brown eyes, holds a beautiful rose

2. Jolly Joseph

"Hi, Paul! Would you like to play soccer with us?" he shouted loudly.

3. Pretty Penny

"When are you going to clean up your room? I asked to you clean it up three times already."

4. Active Annie

Spends most of the time in the library, sits under a tree during recess, practices piano every day for two hours

5. Noisy Nate

Tells lots of jokes, plays practical jokes on friends and family, wears silly hats

6. Serious Susan

Likes to go skating and hiking; cannot sit still in class; climbs trees; wears jeans, sneakers, and a ball cap

0-7424-1803-0 *Building Grammar & Writing Skills*

Name _____ Date _____

Picture It

Use details to describe characters in a story. This helps the reader imagine what the characters like, how they speak, what they feel, and how they behave.

Write a description of a character. Then give your paper to a friend. He or she should be able to draw a picture of the character you described. Ask your friend to include as much detail as possible when drawing the character.

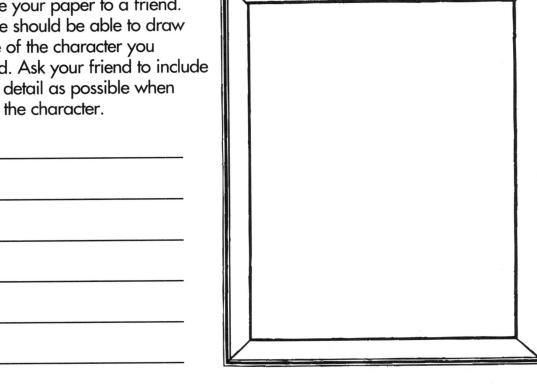

_____

_____

_____

_____

_____

_____

_____

_____

_____

_____

0-7424-1803-0 *Building Grammar & Writing Skills*

Name _____ Date _____

Where Is It?

The **setting** of a story tells where and when the story takes place. It can be a real or imaginary place, near or far away. It tells if the story happens in the past, present, or future, and what time of day it is.

Answer the questions about the setting for each picture.

1. Is this story in a real or imaginary place? How can you tell?

_____

_____

2. Is this story in the past or in the present? How can you tell?

_____

_____

3. What time of day is it in this story? How can you tell?

_____

_____

1. Is this story in a real or imaginary place? How can you tell?

_____

_____

2. Is this story in the past or in the present? How can you tell?

_____

_____

3. What time of day is it in this story? How can you tell?

_____

_____

Name _____ Date _____

What's the Problem?

In every story the main character has a problem. The events in the story show how the character attempts to solve the problem.

Identify the problem in each paragraph. Underline the statement that best describes the problem.

1. Billy was standing in line at the school cafeteria. The hamburgers and chocolate pudding looked delicious! When he took his tray up to the cashier, he discovered his pockets were empty. What happened to the two dollars he had this morning?

    a. Billy had a hole in his pocket.

    b. Billy couldn't decide what to eat for lunch.

    c. Billy lost his lunch money.

2. Matt and Kevin are playing baseball. Kevin hurls a fastball toward home plate, and Matt swings with all his might. Crack! The ball soars over the fence and straight into Mrs. Paulson's living room window!

    a. Matt and Kevin are terrible baseball players.

    b. Matt and Kevin broke Mrs. Paulson's window.

    c. Kevin didn't catch the ball.

3. Dalia got a new puppy for her birthday. He is so adorable! She takes very good care of him. She plays with him, feeds him, and takes him for walks. One day, Dalia couldn't find Cuddles. She looked in his favorite hiding spot under the stairs. Dalia couldn't find him and one of Dad's shoes was missing.

    a. Dalia couldn't find Cuddles.

    b. Cuddles ran away from home.

    c. Cuddles ate Dad's shoe.

0-7424-1803-0 *Building Grammar & Writing Skills*

Name _____ Date _____

What Happened?

The **events** in a story describe all the things that happen.

Read each problem. Write two events that tell what happens as a result of the problem, or two ways the character could solve the problem.

1. Heavy black clouds darken the sky. Travis is walking home without an umbrella.

_____

_____

_____

_____

_____

2. Marcella worked very hard on her book report last night. This morning she was in such a rush to get to school that she left her report on the table at home.

_____

_____

_____

3. Ben's school is having a fundraiser. In order to win the scooter, Ben will have to sell 50 magazine subscriptions.

_____

_____

_____

0-7424-1803-0 *Building Grammar & Writing Skills*

Name _____ Date _____

Solve It

The **solution** in a story is the way the problem gets solved. Sometimes the main character solves the problem. Sometimes the problem is solved in other ways.

Draw a line from each story to its solution.

Sara and Melody are enjoying fishing from a boat. Suddenly, the boat starts filling with water. They search frantically to find where the boat is leaking. They discover a hole in the bottom. A shark must have bitten the bottom of the boat!

It is just the wind from an approaching storm. They get out and fix the tent.

Peter and Tyrone are camping. They set up the tent and settle into their sleeping bags. A huge roar thunders through the tent, and then it collapses. Could it be a bear? Peter gets out to investigate.

She drinks a magic potion that changes her flippers back into feet.

The girls call for help on their two-way radio.

Today is the big game against the Blue Dragons. Nina wakes up and gets out of bed. She falls straight to the floor. Looking down, she finds her feet have turned into flippers.

0-7424-1803-0 *Building Grammar & Writing Skills*

Name _____ Date _____

Begin with a Bang

The **beginning** of a story should be interesting, so the reader will want
to keep reading. Three ways to make your beginning interesting are:

- Ask a question.
- Use a quote.
- Use descriptive language.

Change each beginning sentence. Use vivid verbs or exciting
adjectives to make it more interesting.

1. There is a new student in our class.

_____

2. I have to empty the garbage after dinner.

_____

3. Mexico is an interesting place.

_____

4. Animals live on a farm.

_____

5. The spring carnival was fun.

_____

_____

Choose one of the topic sentences above and finish the paragraph.
Write on the back of this paper.

0-7424-1803-0 *Building Grammar & Writing Skills*

Name _____ Date _____

Catchy Titles

The **title** of a story is very important. It gives a hint of what the story is about without giving away the ending. The title should be interesting enough to make the reader want to read the story.

The first letter of each important word is capitalized in a title. Smaller words, like *in, of, a, the,* or *on* are not capitalized unless they are the first word in a title.

Examples: *Lilly's Purple Plastic Purse*   *The Wind in the Willows*

Read each story. Decide what the story is mostly about. Then write a title.

Title: _____

I found a sea monster! He looked lonely in the dark sea. "I will take him home and love him as my own," I decided. I filled the bathtub with nice, warm water. I even added my rubber ducky so he could have a friend. He splashed and swam as only a happy sea monster could.

When Mom came in she shrieked, "You can't have that in here!" "Why not?" I asked. "Because goldfish belong in a bowl, not the tub." she replied.

What is the story mostly about? _____

Title: _____

Jane sat in a quiet corner in the library. It was the perfect place to work on her report. She was lost in an encyclopedia, when suddenly the lights went out. She ran for the door, only to find it locked. She tried to find a back door, but there wasn't one. Jane decided to call for help. She dialed the fire department. "Surely they can get me out," she thought. But the fire department was busy putting out a fire. Now what? "My mom will know what to do," Jane said. So, she called home and her mother and father came right away. They found a police officer who opened the door to let Jane out.

What is the story mostly about? _____

0-7424-1803-0 *Building Grammar & Writing Skills*

Name _____ Date _____

Facing a Challenge

Journal writing is free writing. It's your chance to write whatever comes to your mind. There are no right or wrong answers. It doesn't have to be perfect.

Challenges are difficult things. We face challenges every day, such learning to ride a bicycle, writing a three-page report, or having a special physical need. When we meet and overcome challenges, we feel very proud of ourselves.

Write about journal entry about a challenge you have faced.

_____

_____

_____

_____

_____

_____

_____

_____

_____

_____

99

Name _____ Date _____

The Best, Most Amazing, Incredible, Wonderful Day!

We all have good days and bad days. Have you ever read *Alexander and the Terrible, Horrible, No Good, Very Bad Day* by Judith Viorst? Alexander was having a really bad day. Write about a really *good* day you have had recently.

It was the best, most amazing, incredible, wonderful day!

_____

_____

_____

_____

_____

_____

_____

_____

_____

_____

_____

0-7424-1803-0 *Building Grammar & Writing Skills*

Name _____ Date _____

Traditions

Family traditions are part of what makes each family unique. Describe a family tradition—a holiday tradition, special occasion, or weekly event.

Remember, a descriptive paragraph gives a description of a topic. It helps the reader "see" what you are writing about.

_____

_____

_____

_____

_____

_____

_____

_____

_____

_____

_____

_____

0-7424-1803-0 *Building Grammar & Writing Skills*

Name _____ Date _____

Unusual Descriptions

Using lots of interesting or unusual descriptive words will make your writing more creative.

Describe a foot without using the words *toe*, *nail*, or *bones*.

_____

_____

_____

_____

_____

Describe your teacher without using the words *nice*, *mean*, *smart*, *pretty*, *ugly*, *good*, *bad*, *hard*, or *easy*.

_____

_____

_____

_____

_____

Describe a winter day without using the words *cold* or *bad*.

_____

_____

_____

_____

_____

0-7424-1803-0 *Building Grammar & Writing Skills*

Name _____ Date _____

Fried Worms on Fridays

Write a letter to your principal about why the cafeteria should serve fried worms for lunch on Fridays.

0-7424-1803-0 *Building Grammar & Writing Skills*

Name _____ Date _____

Silly Story

Use the list of words below to create a silly poem or story. You can change the tense if necessary. Be creative! Your poem or story doesn't even have to make sense!

amble	chase	chilly	conversation	crisp

delicious   discuss   evidence   fun   hot   jangle   jump

lick   lie   magical   mathematics   nervous   path   polite

remember   roar   rude   sing   slither   storm

stubborn   tame   tough   understand   whine

_____

_____

_____

_____

_____

_____

_____

_____

_____

Name _____ Date _____

Personal Poem

Complete the phrases below to help you write a free-verse poem about *you!*
Then write your final poem in the box. **Hint:** Your poem doesn't have to rhyme!

I am _____

I hear _____

I see _____

I wish _____

I feel happy when _____

I feel frustrated when _____

I get angry when _____

I am puzzled by _____

I dream about _____

I wonder _____

I plan to _____

I hope _____

I know _____

I understand _____

I learn _____

I value _____

I love _____

I am afraid of _____

I am embarrassed when _____

I am proud of _____

I am _____

105

Name _____ Date _____

Spring Cinquain

A **cinquain** is a special five-line poem. It does not have to rhyme, but the lines follow a prescribed format.

Line 1: Noun (topic of poem)
Line 2: Two adjectives (describe the topic)
Line 3: Three verbs (actions that relate to the topic)
Line 4: Two more adjectives
Line 5: Noun (another word for the topic)

Spring
Bright, cheerful
Raining, blooming, dancing
Fresh, new
Beginning

Now, try writing your own cinquain! Follow the format above.

_____
noun

_____, _____
adjective   adjective

_____, _____, _____
verb   verb   verb

_____, _____
adjective   adjective

_____
noun

106

0-7424-1803-0 *Building Grammar & Writing Skills*

Name _____ Date _____

Seashore Haiku

Haiku is a form of poetry that originated in Japan. It is usually about nature and does not have to rhyme.

Haiku is formed like this:

Line 1: Five syllables   Soft sparkling water
Line 2: Seven syllables   Bright morning on the seashore
Line 3: Five syllables   Gracious sun warms me

Now, try writing your own haiku! Follow the format above.

_____

_____

_____

Draw a picture to go with your poem below.

0-7424-1803-0 *Building Grammar & Writing Skills*

Name _____ Date _____

Diamond Diamante

A **diamante** is a special poem. It is called "diamante" because it is shaped like a diamond. Diamante poems can be written about any subject.

The diamante has a special format:

Line 1: Noun or pronoun (topic of poem)   Monkey
Line 2: Two adjectives (describe the topic)   Large, small
Line 3: Three verbs (actions that relate to the topic) Swinging, walking, gathering
Line 4: Four-word phrase   Chewing leaves and twigs
Line 5: Three more verbs   Communicating, caring, moving
Line 6: Two more adjectives   Wild, climbers
Line 7: Noun or pronoun (another word for the topic)   Primate

Now, try writing a diamante about yourself, a feeling, or even a science project!

_____
noun or pronoun

_____, _____
adjective   adjective

_____, _____, _____
verb   verb   verb

_____
four-word phrase

_____, _____, _____
verb   verb   verb

_____, _____
adjective   adjective

_____
noun or pronoun

108

                    0-7424-1803-0 *Building Grammar & Writing Skills*

Name _____ Date _____

Laughable Limericks

A **limerick** is a fun type of rhyming poem. It has five lines in a special format. Limericks are usually funny or silly! Look at the format below.

Line 1: Eight syllables   a
Line 2: Eight syllables   a
Line 3: Five syllables   b
Line 4: Five syllables   b
Line 5: Eight syllables   a

There once was a girl who was silly,
She lived in a place that was hilly,
She sneaked out at night,
To fly her new kite,
No more will she cross her Aunt Milly!

Now, you try writing your own limerick!

_____

_____

_____

_____

0-7424-1803-0 *Building Grammar & Writing Skills*

Name _____ Date _____

Autumn Acrostic

Acrostic poems have a special format. First, write a word vertically down the page. Then choose describing words or phrases that begin with each letter of the word.

Light and breezy
Ever flowing in the wind
Autumn dawns
Fall to the ground

Now, try writing your own acrostic poem. Draw a border around your poem to show what it's about.

_____

_____

_____

_____

_____

_____

_____

0-7424-1803-0 *Building Grammar & Writing Skills*

Name _____ Date _____

Fiction

Fiction is a story that is not true. After you have read a fiction book, use this form to respond to what you read.

Title: _____

Author: _____

Write the names of the important characters and two words or phrases that describe each one (think about their physical appearance, personality, or feelings).

_____

_____

_____

Where and when does the story take place?

_____

_____

Briefly outline the plot of the story.

Beginning: What is the problem?

_____

Middle: What events take place to attempt to solve the problem?

_____

_____

End: How is the problem solved? How does the story end?

_____

_____

_____

Compare this book to another book you have read. What is similar about the two stories? What is different?

Illustrate your favorite part of the book. Why was this your favorite part?

Name _____ Date _____

Mystery Cube

A **mystery** story usually has lots of suspense and exciting events. At the end, you get to find out "who done it"!

Follow these directions to make a Mystery Cube:

1. Cut a piece of cardboard (12" x 16½").
2. Draw the outline of the cube as shown below.
3. Cut out the shape.
4. Measure three 4-inch segments horizontally. Draw a dotted line between each segment.
5. Measure three 4-inch segments and one 4½-inch segment vertically. Draw a dotted line between each segment.
6. Fold along the dotted lines.
7. Carefully tape the edges with clear tape.
8. Tuck the flap into the top of the cube.
9. Write the following on your cube:

Top:	Title
Right side:	Characters
Left side:	Where the story takes place
Front:	What is the mystery?
Back:	Three clues that help solve the mystery
Bottom:	Author's name
Inside top:	Solution to the mystery

10. Place some items inside the cube that symbolize the mystery or how it was solved.
11. Illustrate or decorate the cube.

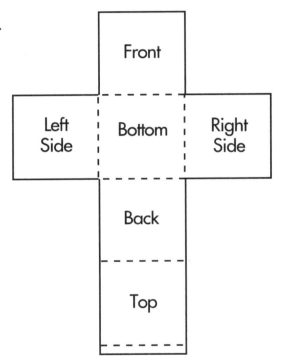

0-7424-1803-0 *Building Grammar & Writing Skills*

Name _____ Date _____

Fantasy

A **fantasy** is a story that contains events, ideas, or even imaginary words that could never exist. Fantasies sometimes contain magic, fairies, dreams, and more!

Write about a fantasy story you have read below.

Title: _____

Author: _____

Who are the important characters in the story?

_____

_____

Where does the story take place?

_____

What problem does the main character face?

_____

_____

How is the problem solved?

_____

_____

What is the magical element in the story?
What things could never happen in real life?

_____

_____

What character would you most like to be? Why?

_____

_____

0-7424-1803-0 *Building Grammar & Writing Skills*

Name _____ Date _____

Biography

A **biography** is the true life story of another person.

Title: _____

Author: _____

Include a picture of the person. It can be a photo or your own drawing.

Person's Name:
_____

What was the most interesting thing you learned about this person?

_____

_____

Give five facts about this person.

_____

_____

_____

_____

_____

Why is/was this person important?

_____

_____

List important dates and events in this person's life.

_____

_____

0-7424-1803-0 *Building Grammar & Writing Skills*

Name _____ Date _____

On the Cover

A **book jacket** helps the reader discover what the book is about. It tells the title, the author, and a summary of the book.

Make your own book jacket about a book you have read.
Cut out the book jacket on the solid lines. Fold it on the dotted line.

Front cover includes:

- title
- author's name
- illustration that represents the theme of the book

Back cover includes:

- summary of the book
  (don't give away the ending)
- short book review

Back Cover	**Front Cover**

0-7424-1803-0 *Building Grammar & Writing Skills*

Name _____ Date _____

Autobiography

Pretend you are the main character in a book you have read, and you are going to write an autobiography. An **autobiography** is a story of your own life. Write as if you are the main character in the story.

This is the autobiography of _____

An important person in my life is _____

He/She is important because _____

_____

_____

_____

_____

An important event in my life is _____

_____

_____

_____

It is important because _____

_____

_____

_____

_____

116

Answer Key

School Days (Page 9)

1. Sam sam takes the bus to school.
2. The the children play soccer at recess.
3. Everyone everyone has fun reading a story.
4. When when will we do a science experiment?
5. Lunch lunch is served in the cafeteria.
6. Our our principal came to visit our class.
7. Students students should be quiet in the library.
8. The the teacher writes the homework on the board.
9. Clean clean your desk before you go home.
10. Have have a great day.

Who's Who (Page 10)

1. i learned that george Washington was the first president.
   I learned that George Washington was the first president.

2. matthew and amelia are doing a project about thomas jefferson.
   Matthew and Amelia are doing a project about Thomas Jefferson.

3. elisa and i are studying about abraham lincoln.
   Elisa and I are studying about Abraham Lincoln.

4. harriet tubman helped rescue many people from slavery.
   Harriet Tubman helped rescue many people from slavery.

5. Many people admire helen keller's courage and intelligence.
   Many people admire Helen Keller's courage and intelligence.

6. Can i write a report about jackie robinson?
   Can I write a report about Jackie Robinson

Wish You Were Here (Page 11)

Dear trudy,
My family and I are in los angeles, california. We have been to hollywood, santa monica beach, and rodeo drive in beverly hills. Tomorrow we are going to visit disneyland. I hope I will get to meet mickey mouse. Wish you were here.

    Your friend,

    roberta

Dear Trudy,
My family and I are in Los Angeles, California. We have been to Hollywood, Santa Monica Beach, and Rodeo Drive in Beverly Hills. Tomorrow we are going to visit Disneyland. I hope I will get to meet Mickey Mouse. Wish you were here.

    Your friend,
    Roberta

It's a Boy! (Page 12)

My baby brother, Nicholas, was born on sunday, september 8, 2002. On saturday, my mom went to see doctor nelson at the hospital. Our neighbors, mr. and mrs. Bigelow, let me sleep over at their house. My mom and Nicholas came home on monday.

My baby brother, Nicholas, was born on Sunday, September 8, 2002. On Saturday, my mom went to see Doctor Nelson at the hospital. Our neighbors, Mr. and Mrs. Bigelow, let me sleep over at their house. My mom and Nicholas came home on Monday.

Geography Lesson (Page 13)

1. Rocky Mountains
2. Lake Superior
3. ocean
4. Kenya
5. country
6. Middle Ages
7. dinosaur
8. North Pole
9. Stone Age
10. river
11. Jurassic Period
12. Nile River
13. Europe
14. state
15. Atlantic Ocean

0-7424-1803-0 *Building Grammar & Writing Skills*

Answer Key

Happy Holidays (Page 14)

1. Did you watch the rose parade on new
   year's day?
   Did you watch the Rose Parade on New
   Year's Day?

2. The librarian helps us choose books during
   national book week.
   The school librarian helps us choose books during
   National Book Week.

3. My family eats turkey and potatoes on
   thanksgiving day.
   My family eats turkey and potatoes on
   Thanksgiving Day.
   The class planted a tree on arbor day.
   The class planted a tree on Arbor Day.

5. Our christmas tree is decorated with lights
   and ornaments.
   Our Christmas tree is decorated with lights
   and ornaments.

6. We watched fireworks at the park on
   independence day
   We watched fireworks at the park on
   Independence Day.

Saturday Matinee (Page 15)

1. Do you want to go to the movies on Saturday?
2. We are going to the theater at the mall.
3. I am going to buy a large popcorn and a bag
   of candy.
4. What do you like to eat at the movies?
5. This movie is great!
6. Meet me outside.

Sentences will vary.

A Birthday Wish (Page 16)

Stories will vary. Check that punctuation is used correctly.

All in a Row (Page 17)

1. Benjamin is wearing a tie, coat, and shoes.
2. Talisa is wearing a swimsuit, hat, and sunglasses.
3. Julia is shopping for pens, pencils, and erasers.
4. She selects blue pens, purple pencils, and
   green erasers.
5. Min is taking a trip to Washington, Oregon,
   and California.
6. He will pack toys, clothes, and books in his suitcase.
7. John, Devon, and Mitchell are going to the
   skate park.
8. Mitchell makes sure to wear his helmet, elbow pads,
   and kneepads.
9. Skateboards, in-line skates, and roller skates are
   allowed in the skate park.
10. My parents, my sister, and I went to the symphony
    hall to see a concert.
11. We heard violins, trumpets, cellos, pianos,
    and drums.
12. Keisha, Sandra, and Travis are at the bowling alley
    for Juan's birthday party.
13. They are eating hot dogs, pizza, cake, and
    ice cream.
14. Juan received a yo-yo, a tennis racket, and a
    soccer ball for his birthday.

My Grandpa (Page 18)

My grandpa had a very interesting life! He was
born on August 20, 1943. He grew up in Boston,
Massachusetts. In January 1963, he moved to Los
Angeles, California. My grandpa lived at 349 James
Street, Los Angeles, California. On June 8, 1964, he
married my grandma at a church in San Francisco,
California. My dad was born on February 1, 1966.

0-7424-1803-0 *Building Grammar & Writing Skills*

Answer Key

The Treehouse (Page 19) ——————————

Dear Donavan,

I can hardly wait to get to your house this weekend. My dad will be dropping me off on Saturday afternoon. We will have fun sleeping in your treehouse. Can we build a campfire?

Your friend,
Simon

Letters will vary. Check for correct placement of commas in the greeting and closing.

Tricky Titles (Titles) (Page 20) ——————————

1. Luis read <u>Number the Stars</u> for his book report.
2. "Stanley the Fierce" is a poem by Judith Viorst.
3. Laura Ingalls Wilder wrote <u>Little House in the Big Woods</u>.
4. Our class sang "America the Beautiful" for the veterans.
5. "The Gift of the Magi" is a story sometimes told at Christmas.
6. Do you know how to play "Happy Birthday" on the piano?
7. "A Girl's Garden" is a poem by Robert Frost.
8. Last week I checked out <u>Because of Winn-Dixie</u> from the library.
9. My dad read us the story "Tom Thumb" before we went to sleep.
10. Our class is reading <u>Sarah, Plain and Tall</u> this month.

A Dog Day (Page 21) ——————————

on october 19 (,) 2002(,) i went to the animal shelter to get a pet(.) my mom drove me to 171 main street(,) huntsville(,) texas(.) we met mr(.) maxwell johnson(.) he showed me cats(,) dogs(,) and rabbits that needed to be adopted(.) what kind of animal should i get(?)

i noticed a small(,) fluffy(,) brown dog sitting quietly in the kennel(.) wow(!) i knew that was the dog for me(.) mr(.) johnson helped the dog out of the kennel, and she ran straight to me(.) what should i name her(?)

Endings may vary.

Hall of Fame (Page 22) ——————————

dear mrs(.) ono(,)

my family and i went to cooperstown(,) new york(.) we visited the baseball hall of fame(.) it was terrific(!) i saw the scorebook from roberto clemente's last game(,) a glove used by hank aaron(,) and a plaque honoring joe dimaggio(.) i thought babe ruth was the most interesting player to learn about(.) did you know he was born in baltimore(,) maryland(,) on february 6(,) 1895(?) i wrote a poem about him called "george the babe(.)" i'll read it to the class when i get back on monday(.)

your student(,)
josh

Tennis, Anyone? (Page 23) ——————————

1. Tennis is my favorite sport.
2. Maurice and I play at the park every Saturday.
3. There are three courts.
4. Each one has a net, a fence, and some lights.
5. My dad bought me a new racket.
6. I need some new shoes, too.

```
T E N N I S G W T O F O D
E F X A I P A R K M W V U
N E Y S H O E S T R O S C
B N N T J R P C T W Z Y K
W C O U R T S D L U N D I
B E K U R S E C I R U A M
Y A R T N E F P G K W D O
B A S X A D Y V H Z E P T
P T E R A C K E T D C W U
Q Y A D R U T A S R L Z C
```

0-7424-1803-0 *Building Grammar & Writing Skills*

Answer Key

Peggy Fleming (Page 24)

Peggy Fleming is a famous figure (skater). She was born in San Jose, California, and began skating when she was nine years old. She won many junior figure skating (competitions) as a (child). In 1964, Peggy competed in the Winter Olympics in Austria. She took sixth place.

Peggy's training in (ballet) helped her develop artistic skating (routines). This helped her win a gold (medal) in the 1968 Winter Olympics in France.

Peggy retired from amateur skating after the Olympics. She became a professional (skater) and toured the (country) doing ice (shows). Now, Peggy is a (commentator) for (television).

Three-Ring Circus (Page 25)

1. elephant (elephants) elephantes
2. box (boxes) boxs
3. drum drumes (drums)
4. clown clownes (clowns)
5. swing (swings) swinges
6. horse (horses) horsees
7. tent tentes (tents)
8. ticket (tickets) ticketes
9. costume costumees (costumes)
10. bicycle (bicycles) bicyclees
11. flash flashs (flashes)
12. announcer announceres (announcers)
13. trampoline (trampolines) trampolinees
14. punch (punches) punchs
15. cannon cannones (cannons)

Many Families (Page 26)

1. families
2. agencies
3. pansies
4. monkeys
5. bunnies
6. therapies
7. valleys
8. pantries
9. juries
10. kidneys
11. babies
12. flies
13. pennies
14. jellies
15. ladies
16. turkeys
17. trays
18. posies
19. journeys
20. jetties

Exceptional Nouns (Page 27)

1. teeth
2. geese
3. women
4. children
5. men
6. moose
7. people
8. deer
9. mice
10. sheep
11. oxen
12. fish

Half a Loaf (Page 28)

1. potato (potatoes) potatos potato's
2. half halfs (halves) halvs
3. mosquito (mosquitoes) mosquitoz mosquitos
4. hero heros (heroes) heros'
5. loaf (loaves) loafs loafes
6. zero (zeroes) zeros zeroz
7. calf calfs (calves) calfz
8. volcano (volcanoes) volcanos volcanoes'
9. shelf shelfs shelvs (shelves)
10. hoof (hooves) hoofs hoofes

Desert Treasures (Page 29)

1. snake's
2. rock's
3. bird's
4. lizard's
5. sand's
6. shrub's
7. tortoise's

Sentences will vary, but check for the following:

8. Kelly's . . .
9. truck's . . .
10. insect's . . .
11. rope's . . .
12. spider's . . .

© McGraw-Hill Children's Publishing

0-7424-1803-0 *Building Grammar & Writing Skills*

Answer Key

Fast Food Fun (Page 30) ———————————————

1. cups'
2. hamburgers'
3. french fries'
4. workers'
5. straws'
6. children's
7. parents'
8. milkshakes'
9. sundaes'
10. fishes'

Sentences will vary, but check for the following:

11. girls'
12. women's
13. hats'
14. snacks'
15. yo-yos'

A Day at the Beach (Page 31) ———————————

Answers will vary but might include:

swimming, building, running, walking, jumping, sailing, eating, playing, talking, laughing, smiling, collecting, surfing, fishing, flying

Being Me (Page 32) ———————————————————

1. My house <u>is</u> brown.
2. My favorite color <u>is</u> blue.
3. We <u>are</u> baking cookies today.
4. I <u>am</u> going to the movies on Saturday.
5. My friends <u>are</u> going with me.
6. What <u>is</u> your phone number?
7. You <u>are</u> standing on my foot.
8. I <u>am</u> four feet tall.
9. The firefighter <u>is</u> driving the engine.
10. Charles and I <u>are</u> playing football.
11. The band <u>is</u> playing "The Star-Spangled Banner."
12. Denver <u>is</u> east of Los Angeles.
13. You <u>are</u> a nice person.
14. <u>Am</u> I your best friend?

Helping Our Earth (Page 33) ———————————

1. Jasmine's family **is** <u>planning</u> a recycling project.
2. They **are** <u>talking</u> to their neighbors.
3. Mr. Chavez **will** <u>look</u> for old newspapers and magazines.
4. The Ong children **are** <u>gathering</u> bags to collect plastic bottles.
5. Jasmine **might** <u>open</u> a lemonade stand to keep us cool.
6. Mrs. Zanuto said she **would** <u>drive</u> us to the recycling center.
7. We **must** <u>respect</u> our planet.

Rainy Day Fun (Page 34) —————————————————

1. It <u>is</u> raining.
   It was raining.

2. Justin and Kendra <u>splash</u> in puddles.
   Justin and Kendra splashed in puddles.

3. Paola <u>plays</u> in the rain.
   Paola played in the rain.

4. Lynda <u>bakes</u> cookies for a snack.
   Lynda baked cookies for a snack.

5. Pam and Arthur <u>watch</u> movies on television.
   Pam and Arthur watched movies on television.

6. Carlos and Keith <u>are</u> at the library.
   Carlos and Keith were at the library.

7. I <u>dash</u> to the barn.
   I dashed to the barn.

8. I <u>am</u> soaking wet.
   I was soaking wet.

Trip to the Mall (Page 35) —————————————

I was <u>invited</u> to a birthday party. So my mom, my sister, and I <u>hurried</u> to the mall to buy a gift. We <u>hopped</u> off the elevator. "Don't touch anything!" Mom said. So, I <u>touched</u> everything. I <u>pulled</u> the sweaters off the tables. I <u>tried</u> on all the hats. I <u>played</u> a game of hide-and-seek with my sister. She <u>cried</u> when I <u>tripped</u> her. I <u>hugged</u> her to make her feel better.

0-7424-1803-0 *Building Grammar & Writing Skills*

Answer Key

We <u>stopped</u> at a candy shop. I <u>licked</u> my lips at the chewy bears. I <u>begged</u> my mom to buy some. She refused. I <u>decided</u> to get my friend some chewy bears. I <u>smiled</u> as the salesperson <u>wrapped</u> the gift. I <u>carried</u> the candy out to the car. What do you think <u>happened</u> to the gift?

Verb Matchup (Page 36)

say	said
grow	grew
bring	brought
know	knew
feel	felt
fly	flew
make	made
find	found
write	wrote
eat	ate
begin	began
leave	left
cut	cut
put	put
read	read
let	let

Shark Tank (Page 37)

1. <u>We</u> went on a class trip to the aquarium.
2. <u>It</u> was filled with interesting sea life.
3. Janice shrieked when <u>she</u> saw the shark tank.
4. "<u>They</u> have really sharp teeth," she said.
5. David reassured Janice, "<u>They</u> can't hurt you."
6. <u>We</u> believed David because <u>he</u> is the tour guide.

In Possession (Page 38)

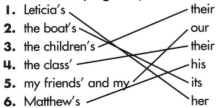

1. Leticia's
2. the boat's
3. the children's
4. the class'
5. my friends' and my
6. Matthew's

their
our
their
his
its
her

Sentences will vary.

Describe It (Page 39)

Answers will vary.

Making Comparisons (Page 40)

1. Margery is the (stronger, <u>strongest</u>) girl in third grade.
2. The blue sailboat is (<u>faster</u>, fastest) than the red sailboat.
3. July is usually (<u>hotter</u>, hottest) than January.
4. Which instrument is the (louder, <u>loudest</u>) one in the orchestra?
5. Turtles are (<u>slower</u>, slowest) than rabbits.
6. Tran is the (funnier, <u>funniest</u>) student in our class.
7. Your slice of cake is (<u>thicker</u>, thickest) than mine.
8. Frogs jump (<u>higher</u>, highest) than mice.
9. Mount Everest is the (taller, <u>tallest</u>) mountain in the world.
10. The summer solstice is the (longer, <u>longest</u>) day of the year.

Sentences will vary, but check for the following:

11. short, shorter, shortest
12. bright, brighter, brightest
13. smart, smarter, smartest
14. cold, colder, coldest

Adventurous Adverbs (Page 41)

Some answers will vary.

1. Sandy <u>happily</u> ate her ice cream cone.
2. Put your backpack <u>there</u>.
3. Milo skated <u>recklessly</u> and broke his wrist.
4. Tyler visited the museum <u>yesterday</u>.
5. When the baby is asleep, we must speak <u>softly</u>.
6. I have soccer practice <u>later</u>.
7. The bear watched her cubs play <u>nearby</u>.
8. Charlotte sings <u>beautifully</u>.
9. Mother decorated the cake <u>carefully</u>.
10. The jellyfish swims <u>slowly</u>.

0-7424-1803-0 *Building Grammar & Writing Skills*

Answer Key

Sports Articles (Page 42)

1. (the, **an**) field
2. (**a**, an) award
3. (an, **the**) ball
4. (**a**, the) wheels
5. (a, **an**) inning
6. (**an**, the) sticks
7. (**the**, a) goalposts
8. (a, **an**) obstacle
9. (a, **an**) umpire
10. (**an**, the) quarterback
11. (**a**, the) outfield
12. (the, **an**) surfboard
13. (**an**, the) team
14. (**an**, the) shin guards
15. (**a**, an) helmet
16. (a, **an**) glove
17. (**the**, an) net
18. (a, **the**) skates
19. (a, **the**) tennis shoes
20. (**a**, an) touchdown
21. (a, **the**) ice
22. (**a**, an) wave
23. (**the**, an) skateboard
24. (**a**, the) water
25. (**the**, a) goggles
26. (**an**, the) scoreboard
27. (a, **the**) spectators
28. (**the**, an) uneven bars
29. (a, **the**) hurdles
30. (**a**, an) time-out

Put It All Together (Page 43)

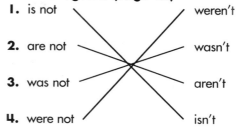

1. is not — isn't
2. are not — aren't
3. was not — wasn't
4. were not — weren't

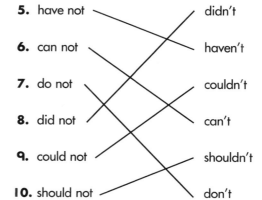

5. have not — haven't
6. can not — can't
7. do not — don't
8. did not — didn't
9. could not — couldn't
10. should not — shouldn't

11. Molly doesn't have any tennis shoes.
12. Brett can't ever find his baseball glove.
13. We aren't doing anything on Saturday.
14. Trent wouldn't ever eat fried worms.

A New Bicycle (Page 44)

1. Mary (receive, <u>receives</u>) a new bicycle on her birthday.
2. She (put, <u>puts</u>) on her helmet.
3. Tony and Jennifer (ride, <u>rides</u>) to Mary's house.
4. Mary (jump, <u>jumps</u>) on the shiny red bike.
5. She (spin, <u>spins</u>) around in the driveway.
6. The friends (<u>laugh</u>, laughs) as they ride.
7. They (<u>race</u>, races) down the sidewalk.
8. The streamers (<u>fly</u>, flies) in the wind.
9. Jennifer (reach, <u>reaches</u>) the finish line first.
10. Tony (finish, <u>finishes</u>) last.
11. Mary (enjoy, <u>enjoys</u>) her new bike.
12. They will all (<u>meet</u>, meets) tomorrow for another ride.

0-7424-1803-0 *Building Grammar & Writing Skills*

Answer Key

All About Giraffes (Page 45)
1. (The giraffe) is a mammal.
2. (Its neck) is very long and muscular.
3. (Its long tongue) is used to pull leaves from branches.
4. (A giraffe) can go without drinking water for more than a month.
5. (Its large, solid hooves) are used to kick predators.
6. (Calves) can stand up 20 minutes after they're born.
7. (It) can live up to 26 years.
8. (An adult male) leads a herd.

Subjects will vary.

The Moon (Page 46)
1. Earth <u>has one moon</u>.
2. The moon <u>revolves around the Earth</u>.
3. One lunar month <u>is approximately 30 days</u>.
4. The diameter of the moon <u>is approximately 2,160 miles</u>.
5. Scientists <u>study craters, mountain ranges, and plains on the surface of the moon</u>.
6. Exploration of the moon <u>began in the 1960s</u>.
7. Astronauts <u>collected rock samples from the moon</u>.
8. Geologists <u>study the rocks</u>.

Predicates will vary.

Match It!(Page 47)
1. e; Parker likes to ride his skateboard.
2. g; The ballerina twirled on her toes.
3. f; My sister's parakeet flew out of the window.
4. d; Our teacher assigned the class lots of homework.
5. a; The amusement park ride was closed for repairs.
6. h; The ice cream sundae is almost too sweet to eat!
7. b; Emily dove into the freezing cold pool.
8. j; The goalie made the save.

Pizza Pie (Page 48)
1. Pizza tastes delicious. **S**
2. Let the dough rise before spreading it out. **S**
3. Dough in the air **F**
4. Anthony pours tomato sauce on the crust. **S**
5. Mom arranges the toppings on the sauce. **S**
6. Mario sprinkles the pizza with red pepper. **S**
7. More cheese **F**
8. We bake the pizza in the oven for 10 minutes. **S**
9. Served hot and bubbly **F**
10. Cut slices **F**

Sentences will vary.

Fun at the Park (Page 49)
1. Sheila wears roller skates, and Andy rides a skateboard.
2. The children play in the park, and the adults watch.
3. Seth buys ice cream, but Karen prefers hot dogs.
4. Fishing is fun, but it is not allowed in this pond.
5. My mom flies a kite, and my dad unpacks the lunch basket.
6. You can eat potato chips, or you can eat tortilla chips.

Katelyn's Garden (Page 50)
Answers will vary, but here are some suggestions:
1. Katelyn cleared the garden. She raked the leaves and collected rocks.
2. Katelyn planted seeds in the spring. She planted beans and pumpkins.
3. The seeds grow quickly. They like warm sunshine.
4. Water helps the plants grow. Katelyn waters them every day.
5. Insects visit Katelyn's garden. Some bugs are good.
6. Pulling weeds is not very fun, but it is an important job.
7. Pumpkins grow very large, and beans grow very tall.
8. Katelyn harvests the vegetables. They taste good.

My Dog (Page 51)
<u>My dog is the smartest dog in the world</u>.
1 Her name is Lulu. **2** She can fetch the newspaper when Dad asks her to. **3** When Mom is sad, Lulu cheers her up by licking her face. **4** I really like it when Lulu helps me find my lost tennis shoe. (Lulu is the best dog!)

Paragraphs will vary.

Answer Key

Tip-Top Topics (Pages 52) ——————
Answers will vary.

Support System (Page 53) ——————
Answers will vary.

In Conclusion . . . (Page 54) ——————
Answers will vary.

Write Your Own Paragraph (Page 55) ——————
Answers will vary.

The Princess (Page 56) ——————
Answers will vary. Accept any adjectives, even if they are unconventional.

Exciting Words (Page 57) ——————
Answers will vary. Accept any adjectives, even if they are unconventional.

Seashore Fun (Page 58) ——————
Suggested answers. Answers will vary:
1. Dad <u>drove</u> the car toward the beach.
   steered
2. The seagulls <u>played</u> at the edge of the water.
   danced
3. Waves <u>broke</u> on the sand.
   thundered
4. Tomas <u>found</u> seashells at the seashore.
   gathered
5. "What's that?" Petra <u>said</u>.
   shrieked
6. "It's a sand crab," Bobby <u>said</u>.
   explained
7. The sand crabs <u>went</u> away when he lifted the rock.
   scurried
8. Sam <u>ran</u> across the hot sand.
   streaked
9. Jessica <u>swam</u> in the surf.
   splashed
10. The beach ball <u>went</u> through the air.
    sailed

The Five Senses (Page 59) ——————
Answers will vary. Accept any adjectives that use the five senses.

Let's Golf! (Page 60) ——————
Golf is a popular sport. Millions of people all over the world enjoy golf. ~~Golf originated more than five hundred years ago~~. People play golf in the United States, Australia, Japan, and Africa. There are more than 14,000 golf courses in the United States alone! ~~Mary, Queen of Scots, played golf a long time ago~~. People can watch professional golfers play on television. It is a sport that men, women, and children can play.

Golf is a popular sport. Millions of people all over the world enjoy golf. People play golf in the United States, Australia, Japan, and Africa. There are more than 14,000 golf courses in the United States alone! People can watch professional golfers play on television. It is a sport that men, women, and children can play.

Careers (Page 61) ——————
Doctors help people get better.
> look into your mouth with a tongue depressor
> give you medicine
> check your ears
> listen to your chest with a stethoscope

Chefs have a very fun job.
> use new ingredients
> taste all the delicious pastries
> create lots of interesting meals
> make food in a big kitchen

Firefighters are heroes.
> put out fires in homes
> rescue people who are in trouble
> take people to the hospital when they are sick

Using a Dictionary (Page 62) ——————
1. Would you find the word gumball on this page? <u>No</u>
2. Would you find the word ginger on this page? <u>Yes</u>
3. What part of speech is the word gill? <u>noun</u>
4. Write the definition for girl. <u>A female child</u>

125

0-7424-1803-0 *Building Grammar & Writing Skills*

Answer Key

Using a Thesaurus (Pages 63) ——————
Answers will vary.

Organize a Web (Pages 64) ——————
Answers will vary.

Organize a Chart (Pages 65) ——————
Answers will vary.

Organize a Diagram (Pages 66) ——————
Answers will vary.

Organize an Outline (Pages 67) ——————
Answers will vary.

Sequencing Sentences (Pages 68) ——————
Answers will vary.

Proofreading (Page 69) ——————

¶Margaret Thatcher was the first female prime minister in Great Britain. A prime minister is like a president. Mrs. Thatcher was born in a town called grantham in 1925. She went to school at the University of oxford. She became chemist Later, she married a man named denis. After passing the bar examination, she became a tax lawyer. Mrs. Thatcher got involved in politics in 1959. She became the prime minister of Great Britain in 1979.

Capitals in the Capitol (Page 70) ——————

the white house was the first official building in washington, d.c. construction began on october 13, 1792. it is located at 1600 pennsylvania avenue in washington, d.c. it is the home of the president of the united states. the president and his family live in one section of the house. every american president except george washington has lived in the white house. the other section is used for the president's office. the white house is a beautiful building.

Perfect Punctuation (Page 71) ——————

"A picnic at the lake is a wonderful idea(!)" exclaimed Mary Jo(.) "I will bring cherry pie(,) ham sandwiches(,) and potato chips(.)"

Patty replied, "Great(!) I will bring a blanket(,) umbrella(,) and lemonade(.)"

"Can I come(?)" Serena asked "I could bring toys and games(.)"

"Sure you can come(,)" Patty said(.) "We'll have lots of fun(!)"

1543 Treetop Lane
Forrester Illinois 56284
July 23 2002

Dear Mary Jo

Thank you for inviting me to the picnic at the lake(.) It was really fun (!) I enjoyed splashing in the lake and riding in the boat(.) Your ham sandwiches tasted terrific(.) I hope we can go to the lake again(.)

Your friend,
Serena

Home-Run Birthday Party (Page 72) ——————
Answers may vary.

All About Birds (Page 73) ——————

¶Birds are unique animals. They can fly, except ostrich and kiwis. Birds hatch out of eggs, and many are born without feathers. Birds have bills instead of mouths, but they do not have teeth. They can cool their bodies while flying through the air or panting at rest. These features make birds special animals.¶There are different kinds of birds. Ostrich are the largest birds. They can be almost eight feet tall. Bee hummingbirds are the smallest birds and are no more than $2\frac{1}{2}$ inches tall. Hummingbirds are the only birds that are capable of flying

0-7424-1803-0 *Building Grammar & Writing Skills*

Answer Key

backward. Penguins use their wings as oars when swimming through water. Woodpeckers drum on trees to create nesting holes and to communicate with other woodpeckers.¶Bird feathers have many different uses. The bright colors can attract mates or scare other birds. Feathers can act as camouflage to protect birds. They help protect birds from cold weather. They are water-repellent on swimming birds. Feathers are important to birds' survival.

Dear Friend... (Page 77)
Letters will vary, but check for correct letter format.

Writing Letters (Page 78)
Letters will vary, but check for correct letter format.

Expository Paragraphs (Page 79)
Persuasive
How-to
Descriptive
Informative

A Horse, of Course! (Page 80)
Answers will vary, but should include the facts listed about horses.

Best Friends (Pages 81)
Answers will vary.

Revising the First Draft (Pages 82)
Answers will vary.

Final Draft (Pages 83)
Answers will vary.

Hula Hoop Fun (Page 84)
6 Let go of the hoop.
3 Bring the hoop up around your waist.
4 Twist the hoop.
7 Keep swiveling your hips.
2 Hold the hoop in both hands.
5 Swivel your hips.
1 Step into the hula hoop.

No School? (Page 85)
Paragraphs will vary.

Old Glory Page 86
1. F The American flag is red, white, and blue.
2. F There are 13 stripes on the flag.
3. O Betsy Ross is the best seamstress in history.
4. F The 50 stars represent the 50 states in the United States.
5. O Red is the best color.
6. F Our school displays an American flag.
7. O Everyone should have an American flag at home.
8. F "The Star-Spangled Banner" is our national anthem.
9. O Whitney Houston sings the national anthem better than anyone.
10. F The national anthem is sung before all professional sporting events.
11. O "Old Glory" is a good name for the American flag.
12. O The American flag is a symbol of liberty.

Carpool (Page 88)

Beginning: Introduces the characters and the setting	She hauled the jack and spare tire out of the back and changed the tire. We were soon back on the road and made it to school just in time for the bell.
Middle: Tells about the problem and events	Early Monday morning, Mom was driving the carpool to school. The three of us were sitting in the back of the van.
End: Solves the problem and closes the story	All of a sudden, thump! Mom quickly swerved off to the side of the road. Jumping out, she discovered a flat tire.

© McGraw-Hill Children's Publishing   0-7424-1803-0 *Building Grammar & Writing Skills*

Answer Key

Story Organizer (Page 89)
Answers may vary.

Puzzle Planner (Page 90)
Answers may vary.

Colorful Characters (Page 91)

1. Nagging Nellie: "When are you going to clean up your room? I asked to you clean it up three times already."

2. Jolly Joseph: Tells lots of jokes, plays practical jokes on friends and family, wears silly hats

3. Pretty Penny: Has long shiny hair, big brown eyes, holds a beautiful rose

4. Active Annie: Likes to go skating and hiking; cannot sit still in class; climbs trees; wears jeans, sneakers, and a ball cap

5. Noisy Nate: "Hi, Paul! Would you like to play soccer with us?" he shouted loudly.

6. Serious Susan: Spends most of the time in the library, sits under a tree during recess, practices piano every day for two hours

Picture It (Page 92)
Answer will vary.

Where Is It? (Page 93)

1. Is this story in a real or imaginary place? How can you tell? Real, accept reasonable answers.

2. Is this story in the past or in the present? How can you tell? Present, accept reasonable answers.

3. What time of day is it in this story? How can you tell? Daytime, accept reasonable answers.

What's the Problem? (Page 94)
1. c
2. b
3. a

What Happened? (Page 95)
Answers will vary.

Solve It (Page 96)

Sara and Melody are enjoying fishing from a boat. Suddenly, the boat starts filling with water. They search frantically to find where the boat is leaking. They discover a hole in the bottom. A shark must have bitten the bottom of the boat!	The girls call for help on their two-way radio.
Peter and Tyrone are camping. They set up the tent and settle into their sleeping bags. A huge roar thunders through the tent, and then it collapses. Could it be a bear? Peter gets out to investigate.	It is just the wind from an approaching storm. They get out and fix the tent.
Today is the big game against the Blue Dragons. Nina wakes up and gets out of bed. She falls straight to the floor. Looking down, she finds her feet have turned into flippers.	She drinks a magic potion that changes her flippers back into feet.

Pages 97–117
Answers will vary.

© McGraw-Hill Children's Publishing